Acknowledgements

Grateful thanks are due to many people who contributed to the smooth running of life and gave help where it was needed most, whilst I indulged my favourite pastime - writing.

The team of the Obedience Competitor Magazine office, with Jennifer Stretton at the helm, who kept the wheels turning with a minimum of input from me whilst I wrote, re-wrote and put the finishing touches to this book.

Tom Newbould who burnt the midnight oil to painstakingly proof-read every word in the final stages.

Ann Munks who also helped with proofing, but more importantly gave up her own dog's training to video my training weekends, camps and sessions, so that everyone could see people and dogs of all levels enjoying training together.

Pat Leverick, who more than once stepped in to help out at training sessions when the need arose, has been a staunch supporter, and of course catering manager at our training school.

Belinda Pattrick, friend of the highest order, and fellow Leonberger owner, who helped in just about every field imaginable, from child minder to chauffeur, from typesetter to proof-reader, from supporter to shoulder to lean on.

My son Daniel White and husband, friend and 'gopher' Michael White, thanks for being supportive and coping with not seeing much of me during the couple of months preceding publication, and for supplying me with endless hot drinks!

And finally, to all of the handlers who have come along to training sessions, talks, courses and camps, and have listened with an open mind, learnt and enjoyed training with me, but more importantly, found out how to train for competition and at the same time have fun with their dogs. At the end of every course I always explain that I hope everyone has enjoyed themselves, and if I have enlightened just one new person to a dog's way of thinking then it has all been worthwhile.

Happy Dogs - Happy Winners!

The Complete Dog Obedience Manual

The author and son Daniel at the launch in America of her first book
Everybody Can TRAIN Their Own Dog, published by TFH

By Angela White

Dedicated to Michael White

2

About the Author

Angela White is a lecturer in Animal Behaviour, handling and training at Bishop Burton College. She also guest lectures to many fields and at various functions and conferences including speaking to college lecturers and principles, Canine Care evenings, British Institute of Professional Dog Trainers, various clubs, societies, schools etc. in the UK, Europe and America.
She is a qualified Kennel Club Championship Obedience show judge, and holds a Kennel Club breeders diploma, and has gained instructors qualifications with honours with the British Institute of Professional Dog Trainers.

She has successfully competed in obedience competitions up to test C and has also trained dogs for Drug Detection, Working Trials, Agility, Gundog, Security, Show, Demonstrations, and the Media.
She was the first civilian woman security dog handler for the Ministry of Defence.

She operates a veterinary referral service to treat behavioural problems in dogs, cats and other animals. With her husband Michael she runs regular classes, courses, training camps etc., and attracts all levels of clients for dog training from general pet dog control through to championship C.

She has been involved in University research studying the effects of diet on ageing and activity levels, and the effects of stress and testosterone levels. She is currently conducting a study on behaviour of dogs in the society, home and kennels environment.

She is editor of the magazine which dominates Competitive Obedience in the UK, *Obedience Competitor Magazine*, Author of the book *Everybody Can TRAIN Their Own Dog (TFH)*. Author of various educational papers including *College Certificate for Dog Training Instructors and Behavioural Counsellors*. She has other books and papers allied to dogs in the process of being written and published.

3

Tribute

Competitive Obedience in its current form has a lot of people to thank, non more so than the King and Queen of Competitive Obedience, Charlie Wyant and Bing Bellamy.

Both Charlie and Bing became famous for their breeding lines, their phenominal success in the competition ring and their approach to training and instructing.

Bing's super line of characteristically tricolour Border Collies, the very stylish Sealights are famous and still working all over the world.

Charlie's famous Heelaway German Shepherds became legendary in the obedience world, and both Bing and Charlie made up many obedience champions. They went on to teach and influence many of today's top handlers.

It was Charlie who first showed me the importance of *'hearth rug training',* which led to the turning point of taking my own dogs from pet standard to winning in competitions.

The King and Queen of Obedience Bing Bellamy and Charlie Wyant.

Introduction

The approach to competitive obedience training has been gradually changing for the better. It is the aim of this book to bring you up to date with the techniques and attitudes of mind which are open to *anyone* with *any breed* who feels that they would like to enjoy their sport. The techniques are not fancy, nor do they require super human effort, and Olympic style fitness. They do require however, a fair approach, a dog's eye view, a sense of humour, some toys or titbits, patience, the will to succeed and a willingness to relax and enjoy.

Obedience went through a period in its evolution when many handlers were frustrated by the high standards needed in order to win. With frustration comes fear and aggression, very natural responses, ask any psychologist. A positive attitude and sound knowledge however, can change all of this.

Dolphin trainers can teach us a lot. You would never see a dolphin being physically launched through a hoop by his trainer. All of their training is done using rewards. This does not mean that the dolphin is stuffed full of treats. What it does mean is that careful timing of rewards will gradually shape the behaviour of the dolphin to eventually achieve what the trainer wants. There is a gradual progression to the learning process, getting ever nearer to the goal. Of course there will be set backs, but a good trainer ignores these and gets on with the job in hand. A wham bam aggressive approach would never work. Obviously with dogs we can manipulate the behaviour at much closer contact, but still a reward based method of training works the best. It creates in the dog's mind a desire to perform. Without the desire to work, the performance in the ring lacks sparkle and **natural** style. Given the opportunity the dog will choose to 'opt out'.

This book is split into three sections; first the Concepts, second the Techniques, and third Obedience Training and Show Craft. At the start of each section is an index of that section, and at the back is a more complete index which will help you to find any specific subjects.

The best way to use this book is to read the concepts section first. This will help you to understand about your dog, and the way that the techniques should be approached.

The aim is to enjoy, for both you and your dog. Set your sights high, but your daily aims low. To achieve the goals you must proceed with patience, perseverance, a pleasant and controlled frame of mind, but most of all understanding.

The Concepts

Understanding Your Dog

The Dog's Mind

The dog's mind can be likened to a computer. When the computer arrives on your desk, it may be programmed to do certain things, like use power, and put incomprehensible jargon on the screen. Unless you have paid someone else to do the job for you, in order to get the machine to do what you want you have to programme the darn thing. To do this you insert programmes into its memory banks, and this has to be done in a certain way other wise the machine won't understand. Then, when you want to use the said programmes, you have to make sure that you push the right buttons to get the machine to perform! No amount of swearing, cursing and banging will get it to perform without hitting the right buttons in the correct sequence!

How similar our canine friend is. Perhaps it is preferable to liken him to a new garden. A fertile mind ready to be cultivated, plant good quality seed, add a little bit of TLC, and with a bit of encouragement you are there. Plant weeds and that is what you will get, the rubbish of the garden!

The dog goes through various stages of behaviour in his development, which are closely related to the stages that the wolf would go through in his wild state. The most important stage as far as moulding behaviour is concerned is between the ages of four to twelve weeks approximately. This is the socialisation period of the dog's life. His communication skills are well developed and he is interested in everything that comes into his path. At this time he finds it relatively easy to accept any novel experiences because he is genetically programmed to accept whatever his mother says is OK. After this period, if he was in the wild he would be straying from the nest, and so evolution has taught him that anything that he has not met yet may be a potential predator, so he must be wary. We can teach the dog during the socialisation that novel experiences are fun. The more he meets and has *good* associations with the more he will be able to accept throughout life. If this period is not made full use of, then some situations may take a lot of getting used to both for you and the dog.

The domestic canine being a predatory animal comes equipped with the ability to perfect certain skills. His ancestor the wolf shows great skill in hunting, but if we observe the *juvenile* wolf, our domestic dog comes very close to his behaviour. The young wolves practice through play and develop their hunting skills. Our dogs never really go beyond this stage, and we can help them to develop variations on these skills. Play works so well as a motivation because it is the basis that leads to hunting and **food.** Food is the most important thing in a canine's life, closely

7

followed by sex. In other words he is motivated by self-preservation and the instinctive need to perpetuate the species.

Dogs do not understand language, but they do communicate. They communicate through body language mainly and some sounds. They will learn to interpret human sounds, body stance, and even facial expression. At close contact body posture, sound and facial expression can be used. At a distance, sound is more likely to be interpreted, although very clear signals of body posture can be used. The further away you are, the less the dog will be able to read physical signs. Signs and sounds must be very clear, and the same every time in order for the dog to make a connection.

We live in what has become a very aggressive world. Countries and people fighting for supremacy, or simply fighting for their identity. Those who have experienced war now realise that aggression solves very little. The parts of the civilised world that have matured now choose to use communication as their sword. Dog training with aggression likewise achieves very little. The dog does not understand our language, he lives in an alien environment, he is not allowed to follow his natural instinctive behaviours. Treat him with aggression and he will become a nervous wreck, or a hard case who is just waiting to lash out. If he can't hit out at his oppressor, he will redirect his aggression onto something or someone else.

The dog does not have a memory in the same way that we do. He cannot think backwards and forwards, nor does he have the power of lateral thinking. His memory works on triggers. When he sees, scents, hears, or feels something his mind triggers a reaction, and he reacts in a similar way to the last time he experienced the same thing. His brain takes over, he has an automatic reaction, and there has to be a block in his way for him not to carry out what he has been programmed to do. Training or counter conditioning can change this, but the brain will be in conflict with itself, fighting it out between instinctive and learnt

Understanding The Dog's Mind

response. This is where *motivation* comes into play, introduce a good motivation and the dog can learn to act even against inherent instinctive reactions, but the reward must be administered at the right time for him to understand what is wanted. *(See Timing, and rewards)*.

Throughout this book you will be constantly reminded to reward, play and generally enjoy your dog. Your dog should however, learn to deal with adversity, otherwise when faced with it he may well panic, which will result in him running away, fighting, hiding in a corner, or going through a repertoire of displacement activities. The last option is acceptable, as the dog will simply avoid the problem by doing something else. The first three are not acceptable, so we need every now and again to take the dog into situations that might put him under minor stresses and teach him to deal with it. Play, distraction training, food and learnt exercises will help him to focus. Make sure that he is aware of his surroundings and then teach him that it is OK.

The dog can learn in various ways. He can learn by **Observation,** although the dog does not have a good pyramidal system in the brain so this is not one of their best skills. It is seen mostly in younger animals who will watch each other and learn new skills. **Classical Conditioning,** this is the Pavlovian way in which dogs learn from outside stimulus. Pavlov's dogs learnt to get food rewards when they heard a bell. Eventually they salivated at the sound of the bell without even seeing the food. We all play Pavlov in our homes and in our training. Many times we unwittingly teach our dogs, and wonder how we arrived at the stage that we find ourselves. **Operant conditioning,** which basically is the posh name for dog training. Within this scope we can reinforce good or even bad behaviour, by giving positive rewards. We can **Flood** the dog with something to make him blasé about it. We can **Shape** like the dolphin trainers do, getting ever nearer to the goal. We can chain things together each action creating a stimulus for the next thing. We can **Desensitise** the dog to specific actions or sounds. (Many handlers do this by constant nagging at the dog, eventually their voice means nothing).

When the dog reacts to stimuli his mind is trying to justify all of the variables, and he is in conflict between instinct, hormones, learnt responses, bodily functions, and is taking into account environment and atmosphere. All of these things join together and trigger what the brain takes to be the correct response. The dog does not ponder on the consequences, but if his reaction does not get a favourable response he may react differently next time. Without correct channelling the next reaction may be equally wrong in our eyes. So we must take over and show the dog what is wanted, in a way that he can understand and in all situations if we want him to perform well.

If you have learning difficulties and you are off school age, you have a legal right to be taught in a way that you can understand. A dog deserves this right too.

Understanding The Dog's Mind

Think like a dog and you are starting to get somewhere. Once you have mastered the art of throwing away the anthropomorphic view of dogs, teaching them will be child's play.

Starting With A Puppy

Where do you start when you pup is destined for obedience?

If you are lucky enough to be about to start with a new puppy then there are many factors which will have an effect on the ultimate attitude and behaviour of your dog. Moulding the pup in the correct manner can help to prevent problems later on. Much of this moulding is often done quite inadvertently, but if you are not fully aware of the pup's natural development you can mould in the wrong way, not realising that certain problems could have been avoided, whilst other behaviours could have been positively enhanced with the correct start.

The perfect time to be reading this section is prior to getting your new dog, but if you have already got him pick up where applicable. Read through all the sections because this will help you to understand any behaviour that your pup is already displaying, and will also assist you to mould and form a bond with your dog.

Before you buy your pup

Do your home work. A much more important factor than studying bloodlines and winning records is, to look objectively at your proposed animals and discuss, if possible, the lifestyle which has been adopted by owners of these types of dog. Don't be content to just speak to one individual owner, ask several. If possible find someone of a similar age, time allowance and outlook on life as you. Some breeds are highly active and have an extremely strong working drive. Some lines within a breed have more of those characteristics than others. Even some individuals within litters have stronger versions of certain types of behaviour than their litter mates. *'Fast to learn'*, means fast to learn both right and wrong! You have to be sure you are mentally agile and quick-witted, as well as reasonably fit to deal effectively with the sort of dog that may turn out to be a *'work-a-holic'*. On the other hand you may be the sort of person who feels that they have the mental and physical capabilities to live and work with a live wire. Physical and mental strength versus power both physical and mental of a dog is another factor to consider. Dominant type breeds will not suit some people's character, just as submissive types will not appeal to others.

Dog or bitch?

In general bitches are a little easier to deal with than dogs, in that they are not driven to quite the same degree by the need to be in control. Having said that bitches are not an easy push over and I have owned and known many very dominant bitches. Fights between bitches are often more fierce than between dogs. A bitch with a strong character in the right hands will make a very good working dog, because that strength can be moulded in the correct direction. A very dominant male dog can be difficult for the uninitiated to handle, but the same rule applies to both sexes, if you harness the strength correctly it will work for you. If you are just beginning in the field of dog training it will make life easier for you if you choose a less dominant animal.

Once you are sure that you are picking the correct type of dog to suit your personality and lifestyle, then you have to decide where to get it from. The obvious choice is a breeder, but you may wish to help one of the many unwanted puppies by going to a rescue establishment. Unless you go for a specific breed the problem with rescue pups is that you are never quite sure what you are going to get. Choosing a dog tends to be a bit of a lottery, and even with the best advice in the world you can never be 100% sure of what you are going to end up with. It takes experience, a great deal of study, and a bit of intuition to be able to choose the correct dog for you from a litter, or even several litters of pups. I pride myself in being a fairly good 'puppy picker', and based on many years of observations and follow up study on temperament and environment, have in fact chosen and matched puppies to many owners with a high degree of success, both from my own stock and from other breeders, some being pedigree and others crossbreed.

In a perfect world and with the breeder doing his job properly, socialising the litter with other animals, noises, environments, etc., the best age to obtain your pup is around seven weeks old. If you are in the least bit worried about the environment in which the pup is being reared or if he is an only pup, then five to six weeks might be appropriate. BUT you must realise the importance of early social learning and the pup must have the opportunity of learning correct dog behaviour from other dogs in order to be able to happily interact with dogs later on. You must help him to develop his hunting skills through play, just as his litter mates would have done, because you are going to need this natural behaviour to mould your obedience training. He must learn bite inhibition so that he never bites and hurts, he would learn this from his siblings in the normal progression of play because if he bites too hard with those needle teeth, the other pup will withdraw from the game, so in order to keep playing the pup learns to inhibit the force of his bite, a vital lesson for the future days living with humans.

Starting Your Puppy

If the breeder is caring and knowledgeable about behaviour and understands what you are talking about when you discuss these points, then you can quite safely leave the pup with him a little longer to learn more about being a dog, particularly if you do not have the opportunity of early socialisation with other dogs at home.

Dogs, as you know descend from wolves, and are in fact, in their behaviour extremely similar. In the wild situation the den or cave where the young are reared is a relatively safe environment. They therefore have developed an inherent, automatic acceptance attitude to this environment and during the period of their lives accept that they would naturally remain in this safe environment. When they reach the age of around twelve weeks which is when they would, in the wild state be coming out of the safe area, they are genetically programmed, as a defence mechanism to be wary of the new environments, animals and objects that they come into contact with. The reason for this is that in the wild habitat anything that the mother didn't introduce the pup to may in fact be a predator and therefore must be treated with extreme caution at least until proven friendly.

If the dog has not had the opportunity of learning that new things as an item as opposed to new things individually are a fun experience during this early learning period, then problems will, with out a doubt occur when your attempt to teach him that your environment and the objects and animals within it, are safe and enjoyable. That is not to say that it is an impossible situation to sort out, but it is much more difficult, time consuming and testing on your patience. It certainly helps you to deal with the resultant problems however, when you understand the reasons.

Adult dogs who lack the early social learning should be dealt with like puppies, and gently introduced to anything new. You need to be constantly aware of the problem and use play and common bonds akin to the pup's siblings, to help your dog to learn how to deal with new situations. The section on *Distraction training* covers this in detail.

Armed with knowledge of normal dog development you can decide on the type of environment that you want to obtain your pup from, and at what age. If you are determined to have an older pup you must assess his attitude towards new environments, animals, sounds, objects and yourself. Decide whether there are any problems. If so have you the ability, knowledge and facilities to deal with them effectively, and will his attitude have a lasting or recurrent effect on his obedience career? If so does this matter to you? Remember be honest with yourself.

Choosing the Pup

Choosing a pup is never a straight forward process. You must give careful thought to what you actually want and expect. You must try to view the pups at various times of the day if possible, in order to make an objective decision. Some pups may at first appear to be quiet, but you may have caught them after they have just spent an hour playing. To give you an example of this I chose a dog pup for a handler saying that in my view that pup was the best of the bunch for an obedience dog, he was very playful and often awoke before the others and played with toys or me before the rest of the litter were stirring. The prospective owner turned up each evening after work just as the pup was tiring, and finding a cosy corner to go to sleep, and the rest of the pups just were waking up. It took all my powers of persuasion to convince the handler that the pup was a real star. That dog subsequently became a superb Obedience Champion and was Top Obedience Dog of the Year in Great Britain two years on the trot!

What should you look for?

For an obedience dog certain things can be a positive advantage:

a) A people dog, does the pup respond to people as much as he does to the other pups? Does he readily leave his litter mates to come to say hello to you?
b) Voice and sound sensitive, does he respond to your voice, try making differing tones and watch his response.
c) Touch sensitive, we don't want him to jump out of his skin when touched, but on the other hand he should notice and turn to see what is touching him!
d) Movement aware, see if he will playfully follow a small toy, a leaf or a feather. Remember very young pups have difficulty focusing upwards, so wave the article around in front of his nose to get his attention.
e) Playful, he must want to play and readily join in games that are instigated by you or the other pups.
f) Investigative, he should not be unduly perturbed by new introductions into his environment, and after possibly a moment to take it in, should be going forward to investigate.

Choosing a pup for myself (or an experienced knowledgeable and competent handler to work), I would first take into account all of the above factors. Then I would choose from the most likely puppies, eliminating any that just didn't appeal to me because of appearance or just plain gut feeling, the most dominant one. Dominance can be identified in the one who instigates games, the one who the others give in to, the one who is at the feed bowl first, and stands his ground, the one who plays hunting games like waiting in ambush, pouncing, standing over his siblings etc. This pup whether male or female will make a good basis for you to create the type of working dog that you want, keen, lively, outgoing, yet biddable with sensitivity.

Choosing a pup for someone just starting, for a child, for a less agile, or less knowledgeable person, I would again consider the first factors but then would definitely **not** choose the most dominant one. I would go for the quieter, more inclined to cuddle pup. Try this test; pick up the pup, handle him positively and with care, turn him on his back and see if he accepts this restriction, if he struggles immediately and vigorously he may not be the pup for less experienced hands. All pups will eventually wriggle, but if they more inclined to accept your manipulation this is a good sign, particularly for the novice.

Taking Your Pup Home

Before you go to collect your pup decide where he is going to sleep, where he will spend his days, and have food, toys and blankets ready for his arrival. It is important that you establish a bond with your pup. If you have other dogs in the household, obviously you will want the pup to spend some time with them, but on the other hand he must learn to be alone sometimes, to play with you and that the fun and games do not come solely from the other dogs. Therefore if he is to live indoors a crate or indoor kennel will be a good investment. The security will give him a safe environment away from the hustle and bustle of the house, and will double as an ideal travelling cage.

If the dog is to be kennelled, then it is best if he can have his own individual kennel and run. By having this arrangement you are able to control the dog's development much more, and he will learn to follow your lead because of your control which is executed in the kindest possible way. Your dog will know where he stands, and that you are in control. Obviously you must not leave the pup crated or kennelled for hours on end, he is a social animal and needs company in order to develop correctly. The crate gives him a retreat where he can safely go out of harms way if he wishes or when you decide the time is right, when he is tired, when you go out, or when you are too busy to concentrate on him and prevent him getting into mischief. This control will help to make him grow into a well adjusted individual.

Crate and kennel training is relatively simple, it is a matter of waiting until the pup is very tired, or he is hungry, or he wants to have a good chew and then just pop him in with the appropriate item, i.e. blanket, food or chew bone. Often a cover over the crate or an enclosed area of the kennel will make the pup feel more secure. A quiet setting for the crate or kennel is good idea so that the pup does not become distressed watching activity going on outside. Build up the time he is enclosed, and always give him a treat as he enters the crate or kennel some pups adjust quicker than others. Sometimes sitting with him until he settled works best, for others it works better if you leave quickly to start with so that he can't see you, but work back to the situation where he is in his crate or kennel and is content to stay there whilst you carry on your business outside. A supply of his favourite chews or biscuits often do the trick teaching him that it is rewarding to be in his own environment, most of all be patient.

Taking Him Home

The journey home may be your pup's first ever trip anywhere. Consider the trauma. Isolated from your family, strange people restraining you, you are placed in a moving environment, strange smells, strange shapes, strange feelings, in fact just about everything is strange and new. The competitive obedience dog will spend a lot of time travelling around the country in cars or vans, so don't make that first journey a severe trauma. Ideally let someone else drive you so that you can concentrate on the pup. Take along plenty of towels in case he is sick, nervous tummies are very common in young pups. You are very fortunate if the pup doesn't have a *little accident* of some sort. If you have been going to view the pups on a regular basis you will not be completely strange to the pup. Hold him gently but firmly and talk in a soothing voice, stroke him and help him to accept this frightening experience. A familiar smell can be of help, a piece if bedding from the breeder, even if it is one that you have supplied previously, to absorb the smell of the litter, will provide a familiar scent to help the pup.

The New Lead and Collar

All dogs who are to live in a human environment must wear a collar and identity tag, and of course we need an anchor to which we can attach our arm extension - 'the lead'. Puppy collars should be soft and gentle, a soft webbing or nylon with a buckle fastener is ideal. Avoid hard bulky leather to start with, although the next collar which you purchase for him may be good quality bridle leather if you wish. Certainly avoid chain or any other harsh material as these are totally unnecessary, and may damage the pup's tender neck and vertebrae. Some pups will react in an extreme manner to the first time they have something around their neck. Remember that the neck area is where another dog or animal would attack them and so they may react as though they are being attacked. As always be patient, leave the collar loose and distract the pup with a game or chew until he realises that the collar does not pose a threat.

Once the pup has become accustomed to the collar and had a few days to adjust, try attaching the lead. Choose an appropriate soft leather, webbing or rope lead, with a safe trigger hook fastener. Again you may get an adverse reaction, but distract and play with him allowing the pup to drag the lead around and he will soon come to accept it.

Now you can start to teach the dog to enjoy the lead, producing toy and lead at the same time, hold on to the lead whilst you play with him. Every so often he will become restricted by the lead, distract and encourage him back towards you with the toy. Soon the pup will see his lead and know it is playtime. This attitude will be extremely useful when you start to mould his play into obedience exercises.

Building a Bond

You must make the first few days of the dog's new life with you as happy as possible. He must learn that you are someone that he can trust at all times. Take control of his life and start as you mean to go on. Provide him with a safe haven to sleep in and put him there when you know that he is tired. Produce toys and play with him when you know he will be playful, and feed him when you know he is hungry. Notice the way that I am approaching the subject putting you in control all of the time. This is how you and every dog owner should begin and indeed carry on throughout the dog's life. Don't wait for him to instigate behaviours, you must control his lifestyle. This approach will be beneficial in two important ways, firstly you will prevent your dog becoming dominant over you, dominance is the most common behavioural problem that I am consulted over when I don my hat of applied animal behaviourist. Secondly your dog will look to you all the time as his team leader, and will be constantly checking with you that he is on the right track.

Play for an animal of predatory background like a dog is one the most important features of learning. His reasons for living at the very basic level are food and sex, i.e. self preservation and to perpetuate the species. His hunting skills are naturally learnt whilst he is still in the litter with his brothers and sisters. We normally take him away from this a little early and so we must continue to develop these skills and of course now we can channel them into the types of skills that will be useful to the dog's obedience career later on. Play works in development and training as a reward because of this very basic link to survival. It is the primary skill for hunting, hunting means food, food means survival.

Like children, dogs benefit from *'Quality time'*. Time spent nagging and getting annoyed with the pup will be counterproductive. Time spent in positive play, socialisation and environment exploration will be of far more benefit to you both.

How to play with your pup is covered in the section on *'The Want'*, and this section will also help you to develop some of the skills needed to form a bond.

A bond is all about trust and enjoyment. If you control your dog and his environment you will be able to trust him because you will learn to predict his actions. If you are fair and do not try to trick your dog he will learn to trust you. In order to reap most benefit from these early days you need to learn about *'Understanding the Dog's Mind'*, *'Motivation'*, *'Timing'*, and *'Play Training'*, all of which are covered in the concepts section.

The more you understand your dog, and learn to implement that understanding, the more he respects and trusts you, the greater the bond. Work with your dog until you know how he will react in any given circumstance, expected or unexpected. Play with him until you can turn him onto *'play mode'* at any time and anywhere. Handle, groom and massage his body until he readily accepts your touch and enjoys it. Continue this throughout his life to maintain your relationship in tip top condition.

'The Want'

The 'Want' is not about *you* wanting to win a ticket or even to just win out of Beginners, the 'Want' is the mental and physical condition that you need to develop in *your dog* so that each time you use a key word like 'Watch', or 'Heel', or 'Retrieve', the dog says in no uncertain terms, 'Yes please, I want to work with you'!

All dogs are different of course and the degree of power behind this yearning will be variable. If you have a more sensitive, or quieter type dog he may not be in such a hell bent fury to get into the heel position. But, having said that all training should be aimed at teaching the dog to enjoy and therefore develop, in ever increasing degrees, the 'Want'.

This can only be achieved by teaching *yourself* how to keep the dog interested and excited in everything that you try to achieve. Even if you carry out a sequence of training an exercise incorrectly, if the dog has the 'Want', then you can laugh and start again. The dog will not be unhappy and you will not have spoilt his spirit, as long as you have not lost your temper and blamed the dog for your error. Bear in mind that if the dog behaves incorrectly then your training methods, and most importantly, your timing should be carefully scrutinised. Do this and you will make a far better trainer in the long run. Those who think that the dog is wrong should look carefully at themselves. The dog is being taught these exercises, which on the whole are most unnatural, from the so called intelligent animal at the end of the lead. A bad teacher will produce an ill prepared pupil! There is nothing natural for a dog about walking to heel, sitting straight, or performing multiple position changes for no apparent reason. So, to teach these things you must

The dog must learn to 'Want' to work with you, note the happy open mouthed expresion on Smudge's face.

gain the confidence and trust of your dog and teach him to enjoy learning new things and to perform with exuberance and accuracy the old ones.

But, I can hear you saying, how do I teach my dog to *'Want'?*

Well for some it comes more easily than it does for others. Even the very keen lively types of dog need to be channelled into *wanting* what you *want*! Teaching your dog to play is a very important factor, but you must observe and react from the dog's point of view and be sure that he realises that he is playing and interacting with you and not just with a toy.

The importance of learning to read your dog can not be emphasised enough. Learn to anticipate your dog's actions then, steer him away from undesirable traits, and encourage him whole-heartedly in the things that you want him to do. It never ceases to amaze me how I can very accurately guess how other people's dogs are going to react in a given situation, just by watching the dog with their handler for a few moments; and yet, the handler in question is taken completely by surprise by their dog's actions and reactions time and time again. You must learn to think about your actions and those of the dog. If your dog always reacts in a certain way and this is not what you are aiming for, then you must be doing something (or failing to do something) which makes or allows him to react so.

How to get the 'Want'

Achieving the *'Want'* should be a carefully planned yet natural procedure, making sure that you are always in a position to help the dog to enjoy and be confident at each and every step. The chapters on *play training, toys, motivation and timing* will help you. Assuming all of these chapters have been read and thoroughly understood, then you can start your daily routine to teach your dog to *'Want'*. Even if you think he is already keen, it will be worth following a set routine to make sure he really *wants* what you think he *wants*. It can take time and a dog on which mistakes have already been made will take longer than a young dog at the outset of his training.

All of this initial training can be done in the comfort of your own front room, or a quiet corner in the garden. So long as you and the dog are comfortable and confident in your surroundings then it's fine. This point is an important factor in the training procedure, the surroundings must not be frightening or distracting, at least not to start with. Having decided upon your location then you may commence your training according to the following stages:-

The 'Want'

Step one- First the dog needs to enjoy being on the lead, we will teach him to *'Want'* to be on the lead. If he doesn't like the lead, then over a period of time you need to do pleasurable things like feed him his meals, and play with him whilst he is on the lead. Eventually with patience he will come to associate the lead with pleasure. With dogs who have already gone through the sort of harsh, old fashioned heel check training procedure, this simple start of training on the lead may be a major stumbling block as the lead may be an immediate turn off to the dog. So here again you must **read your dog.** If the dog is unhappy or frightened then treat him like a puppy; sit or kneel down on the floor, or at least come down to dog level and let him trail his lead whilst you feed him his meals or titbits; play with your hands or simply have a cuddle, everything you can think of to help build a trust bond. Take your time and be patient eventually his confidence will build. He must learn by your good handling and fair attitude that nothing horrible is going to happen just because he is on lead. In fact he must realise that much pleasure can be derived from the lead and the *new you.*

Read your Dog, and only move on to the next stages when you are sure he is becoming happy and confident. If you have a young puppy, then this can be your first step, playing and cuddling on the floor, gently introducing little playful tugs on the lead to bring him towards you for pleasure and security. Tease him with a toy or knotted rag, keeping hold of the lead all of the time so that the dog is never far away from you. Encourage the dog towards you continually by bringing the toy or play close to your body and following it up with lots of cuddles. You are now using the lead as an extension to your arm, and never should any aggression be forthcoming if you want your dog to enjoy being trained, to enjoy being by your side, and to *'Want'* to be a team with you.

Step two - Progress with a few short sessions like this each day, never going on too long so that the dog becomes bored, and reading your dog so that you always leave him *'wanting'* more. You will soon see the first stages of the *'Want'* develop.

It is important to realise that all dogs are different, and there can be no set time limit on training and developing a bond. Much depends on your ability to read your dog, to get your timing right, and indeed how many negative factors like bad training or loss of temper have gone on in the past. It may be a case of making your mind up to be a new person in your attitude towards your dog, and then convincing your poor canine friend that you have changed. As one enlightened young woman on one of my summer camps proudly proclaimed to her dog "You've got a new Mummy!"

Step three - The next stage of the training procedure is to be that same trustworthy person in a different place or environment, to once again win your dog's confidence, and then induce enjoyment and fun in all circumstances. This is particularly important if you are training a pup or re-training an older dog. He needs to know that things can be fun with you in every situation, and that varying environments are not to be feared or found too distracting. So choose another quiet place, maybe another room in your house, or any familiar area, and start the training again, from the beginning. Remember your top aim is to teach your dog to 'Want' to work in all situations, at any show, anywhere in the country, and not to find other external factors more stimulating, more rewarding or even just more comfortable and less boring. The dog must be happy and contented with you everywhere and so you must teach him that you are the best thing since sliced bread in any situation!

Developing this bond is the most important thing you will ever do, so take your time and make sure each step of the way the dog learns to trust and want to be with you. This is not a time for lapsing into long stretches of heel work or going through any other exercises which you may have already taught. It is a time for bonding, trusting and learning to play together as a team.

Once you are confident that you have achieved this you can then start to incorporate a few key words, together with gentle guidance into physical actions, that the dog will learn to respond to automatically later on. Once again if you have made mistakes in the past or if you know you always get a submissive reaction to certain words then now might be the time to change some of those words. If in the past for instance, your dog has been yanked or harshly checked into the heel position on the command *'Heel',* then it might be easier for you to change to another key word like 'close'. The fewer bad associations the dog has the easier it will be for you as a trainer to help your dog to enjoy his work.

Step four - To start to incorporate formal teaching into the 'Want' probably the easiest word and action to start with is *'SIT'.* Making sure you have a hold of the lead, play with the dog in front of you, (sit or kneel on the floor if you are teaching a puppy or small dog because you don't want to over power him). Then, when the dog is in a good position for you to easily place him into the sit position, do so, simultaneously giving your 'sit' key word. Use a titbit or your toy in your right hand positioned above his head to motivate and angle him back into position. *(See Stays - Sit).* You should *not* say to yourself, 'Right I'm going to sit him now', and attempt to do it. You should relax in to the situation and place him only when you know that you can get a good and positive result without being harsh or rough with the dog. Even if it takes a little longer for you to get yourself organised, a natural and unforced approach will reap much better and more confident results than a fumbled awkward manner. Just keep the dog in position for a very few seconds and then release by introducing a key word that will in the future tell him that he can relax, I say 'OK'. By introducing a word to say to the dog that you've finished there is never any doubt in the dog's mind whether he should be still sitting there. By removing doubt you are looking to a future with a confident accurate dog.

You still have the dog on lead of course during these sessions, and you continue to play, cuddle and instil confidence and pleasure. You must work together as a team, and build on the bond which will give you the *'Want'*. Don't, just because we have introduced a key word, become all formal and revert back to your old rigid ways, keep your training light with fun. There should be no difference in yours or the dog's attitude whether playing or carrying out exercises. Gone is the 'Let him know he's working' attitude. This has been replaced by a situation that is fun and enjoyable and so instils confidence in you and the dog, and indeed to all who observe from outside.

The attitude and theory applied in teaching the *'Want'* can be adopted in teaching all exercises, and each individual training exercise is covered under it's own section within the book later on. Developing the *'Want'* by means of trust building, bonding, reward and play will help you in all of your training. It will teach you how to read your dog and even if it takes time you will find that it is worth persevering and this will save months if not years of heartache and frustration later on.

Diane Clarke uses her 'Want' aid to get Abbie's attention for the 'Watch'.

23

Fun and Enjoyment

It is pointless entering into a sport as a free time activity or even as a way of life, if you are not going to enjoy it, you may as well have stayed at home and bred gerbils or taken up flower arranging. Both of which I'm sure are fun, but my message is that if training and competition work is what you have chosen, then make up your mind to enjoy every minute.

The very fact that you enter a competition indicates that you would like to win or at the very least, achieve some degree of success. This does not have to be achieved with a heavy rod approach and, as I hope you will appreciate especially after you have read this book, training and competing should be and can be fun for both you and your dog. Of course there are times when you will be tense, like those times when you are leading your class with scent or stays to do, or those occasions when you feel that you stand a good chance because the particular judge whose class you are in likes your style of dog. But, you should not let

Holly is a super stylish Pyrenean Sheepdog having fun here with 'mum' Yvonne Hollyoak from Belgium

your nerves or your desire to win get in the way of your good principles, nor take over to the detriment of your dog's mental or physical well being. There is always another show, and if you want your dog to remain consistent, you must take these things in your stride, particularly if you want to stand a good chance of winning next week as well. Good dog trainers learn to keep calm at all times, some even take yoga to help maintain the equilibrium.

In schools nowadays, children are taught with a friendly approach. Corporal punishment has long been a thing of the past. It has been proven that more children learn quickly and thoroughly given a positive and motivated background than was the case with a more negative attitude. The more laid back and gentle

24

Fun and Enjoyment

approach incorporating play with learning, brings out the individuality and confidence in young children.

Likewise corporal punishment should be ruled out for dogs. It makes even less sense in the case of dogs, because of the type of memory a dog has, he rarely connects the punishment with the crime. *(see Understanding your dog)*.

So let us enjoy our friend the dog. Take time to understand his abilities and limitations. Teach through play and give motivation. Give the dog reason to want to be with you and create a team spirit.

Making competition work fun for both dog and handler shows the onlooker something worth watching. It promotes the sport and gives it meaning and credibility. No one likes to see animals under pressure or unhappy, so practise what you preach and keep it fun, and then sit back and watch the positive reactions.

All exercises - without exception - can be taught with a caring, no force, fun approach, and to a standard that will glow amongst the best. Understand your dog, don't be afraid to stand back and watch something that is not quite correct, because by doing this you can find for yourself new ways to make understanding the exercise easier and more fun for both you and the dog.

When things go wrong analyse and be objective. Teach with patience, care and motivation. The dog will follow what he thinks is the correct course of action, it is up to you to guide him into what you want. When he goes wrong, stop and ask WHY? Count to ten and go back to the drawing board. Most of all remember the dog did not ask to get involved, he's there because you want it to be so. Treat him with respect, and enjoy one of the most rewarding relationships known to mankind.

Timing

Perfect timing *can* mean the difference between teaching the dog what you want to achieve - and teaching the complete opposite! Yes, it can be, and often is, as crucial as that.

I'm sure that you can all think of friends, acquaintances or even times when you yourself have struggled week after week, month after month, sometimes even year after year, trying to teach the dog certain exercises with only negative results. Often despondent, handlers give up in desperation, ask someone else to teach the dog for them, or worst of all give up on the dog all together, passing him on to some one else, labelling him stupid. Although I state that the last statement is worst of all, perhaps in all honesty the dog will actually be better off in more caring and sympathetic hands!

One of the exercises that causes most problems is the retrieve. Many handlers struggle needlessly through lack of understanding or incorrect application of timing. Other exercises seem to be blundered through over a period of time, without good timing the results are not as perfect as the handler might like, but if he gets it right enough of the time, the dog starts getting the message, of sorts! Blunder unfortunately is not so productive on retrieve. Retrieve is a complex task requiring the many different parts to be perfected. Incorrect timing can often result in the exact opposite of what the handler is trying to achieve. More precise details are given in the section on retrieve but this particular exercise is the perfect example to illustrate the importance of timing.

Remember the way the dog's mind works - he is thinking of what is happening to him **NOW**. Imagine yourself in the dog's place; your human prises open your mouth, pops in this 'thing', and says 'Hold'. He then takes it out of your mouth he might say 'Give' at the same time, you release the article and he says 'Well done Good Boy' in a pleasant tone. So, the next time he again pops the article in your mouth it triggers your reaction for reward which is SPIT IT OUT! You step back wagging your tail, waiting for the praise which must surely follow. Your human then goes into one of his rages, 'Bad dog, Stupid dog!' he says.   What an unpredictable human you have. Eventually he calms down and tries again, this time you try even harder to give it up quick, the human goes frantic. Perhaps the human does not want you to take the article at all, after all nothing pleasant has ever happened when it has been in your mouth! So the next time you turn your head away trying to avoid the nasty object, clamping your mouth tight shut, you didn't particularly like it any way, and absolutely no pleasure can be associated with it. The human tries to catch hold of your mouth, and ram the article in, you clamp shut - it has worked, the human walks away muttering something about

Timing

tomorrow. Well at last you have got the idea, the human wants you to totally ignore the nasty thing! No problem! A perfect example of how by praising at the wrong time, the dog can totally misinterpret your actions. Think how you could teach your dog NOT to retrieve, it is not so far away from the above description that is seen going on all over the country under the inappropriate title of training.

So when teaching any exercise praise, motivation and encouragement must come at the very time the dog is performing correctly, or when he is showing signs of understanding what is required. When teaching something new or progressing on a part trained exercise the encouragement **must** coincide with the guidance into the action to achieve the required results. It is too late afterwards, even half a second afterwards is too late. Remember the dog relates the reward, praise, or chastisement to what he is doing **NOW**.

This can be rather a difficult concept for humans to understand. Our powers of forward and backward and indeed sideways thinking are most advanced, but because of our powers we are able, with a little practise to understand to some degree how a dog perceives the world. Once we have good understanding, dog training comes very easily to us.

It is a good idea to practise getting your timing right on an inanimate object. I often demonstrate using a puppet, *Oscar*, so as not to put a dog through the misery of mis-handling. You can practise by pretending your left hand is the dog's mouth and placing the article for him to hold in your hand. See how hard it is to get your timing perfect, especially if you've been getting it wrong for a long time. It takes practise but it is better to get it right without the dog. The secret is to make sure that what your are rewarding is the bit you are trying to teach. This concept can then be transferred to all exercises.

The speed at which your dog will learn from the new you will be dramatic. Your dog can be taught many new things, test exercises and tricks just for fun. Each task is approached in the same attitude of mind, perfect timing, motivation, fun, and a clear idea of what you are trying to achieve. The end results will be exciting, satisfying and fun for both your and the dog.

Motivation

In order to carry out given tasks reliably, and to learn new tasks, your dog needs to be sufficiently motivated. Just like us the dog works to gain enjoyment, or at the very least relief, as a reward for his actions. Without motivation we can end up with dogs who 'turn off', or indeed never 'switch On'.

Food and play are directly linked because, as with most predatory species, play is the natural way of learning about life and to hunt for food. So the same survival instinct is driving both the need for food and the want to play. This is why these two motivational tools are the best to use in training. *(See the sections on play training and rewards.)*

Motivation can develop in many ways; praise from you, by reward such as a titbit or a toy; or just from the sheer enjoyment of carrying out a task that the handler has taught the dog to enjoy. Some dogs need far more motivation than others, but all will respond favourably, when motivation is delivered at the correct time and in a way that the dog can connect with the given task. Motivational aids are useless in teaching, if given at the wrong time, as the chapter on timing explains in detail.

A dog can be taught to enjoy all sorts of tasks, with correct and timely use of motivation; but motivation must be given in a way that the dog can understand, he needs to learn that every segment of what you are teaching is fun. If

*Daniel motivates Spottie with titbits and sheer **fun!!***

every segment is fun, there is no need for his bodily instincts to take over in the search of release from boredom, apprehension, frustration or even fear. Without the correctly channelled motivation, the very release from a boring or frustrating action can be motivation enough for him to follow that same pattern of behaviour the next time, (i.e. strive for the release); and therefore he will learn an action which is not what you were trying to achieve.

If things do go wrong, for instance if you are teaching a new exercise and the dog is not showing any signs of understanding within a few minuets, then stop and think carefully. Is your method of training correct for what your are trying to achieve? Is your timing right, (i.e. are your actions and reward in the right place)?

Motivation

Last but not least are you motivating him sufficiently, is there reason for him to 'W*ant'* to perform?

Motivation is what makes the world go around. For some, motivation can come from just the basic need to survive, but for most it gives a reason to go on. We as humans are motivated to work, our motivation being to earn money on which to live, feed, clothe and house our families; and hopefully have enough at the end of the day to provide for recreation, (get to the odd dog show perhaps)! In some cases our jobs provide motivation in themselves, giving us the desire to strive to achieve our aims. For animals like our dogs, who do not possess the power to look ahead in that manner; nor possess the mental ability for lateral thinking; and deprived as they are of the basic motivational need to provide food, (it is always provided for them in a convenient dish by us); then motivation must be stimulated from things that the dog can enjoy. Pleasurable contact with humans or other animals; toys, titbits or tasty morsels, games, etc. Because we are the provider of the food and safe accommodation the dog as we know it never quite grows up. He maintains a puppy like out look on life. In the natural development of most predatory animals, play has a big role in the development of the puppy. In a captive situation play is an ideal tool for motivation. *(See play training)*.

The ball is often a favourite with Border Collies like Sue Brinkley's Flynn

Motivation is one of the keys to a reliable, happy, no hang ups dog. As handlers striving for perfection, we can become very repetitive and boring if we are not very careful. Picture the scene; a handler is teaching his dog to walk to heel for the competition ring. He starts off by giving the dog a check and saying 'heel'. The dog walks by his side, nothing startling but it is OK. The handler proceeds to march up and down saying 'Heel, Good boy. Heel good boy'. The dog remains in the heel position. At the end of the training session the handler is relatively pleased with his dog and follows the rule of 'Praise your dog' at the end of the exercise. Then he releases the dog and allows him to 'Do his own thing', or puts him back in to the car. Feeling that he was successful in his training the handler repeats the procedure at the next training session, and then the next, and so on. Being a creature, like us, that aims for self preservation or pleasure, the dog soon starts trying to eliminate the boring bits and get to the interesting bits. Even if it is a physical impossibility to get away from the boring bits the dog will go into auto pilot, *'switching off'* until the good bits come his way. Reward, in the dog's eyes, comes only at the end of the exercise so that is what he feels he should try to get to. Even if the reward is only release from the monotony or boredom, it is worth aiming for if there is nothing else. At this stage of the proceedings the handler may become annoyed and violently check, chastise or even hit the dog. This may result in attention of sorts from the dog, most animals would watch if out there was a fear of something or someone getting them. But, for how long? At the first available opportunity, if it was you, you would be off out of it as soon as possible, and so will the dog. The dog has been systematically trained, all be it inadvertently, to switch off from the handler in heel work, and yet come alive at the end when he's finished. The result is the exact opposite of what the handler was trying to achieve. The dog like us is programmed to react in certain ways, and the more we understand about this, the better dog handlers and indeed the better people we will become. *(See The Doggy Mind - understanding your dog).*

Choosing your Motivational Aids

Motivational aids can come in many guises. Food being the basic need to survive, rates top of the list as a motivator; but be careful when using food, it must never be seen by the dog to have run out. You must not give to much to upset the dog's diet or sicken him so that he turns off. The chapter on *Timing* explains how to use your rewards and motivational aids in the correct way. Toys are a superb way of building a bond and getting a dog highly motivated, but again you must understand the limitations and usage before going blindly ahead, *(see play training)* and spoiling a potentially excellent motivational aid. When you produce your motivational aid it does not automatically mean that the dog understands what you are trying to achieve, but it does mean that he is happy and has something worth aiming for. It gives him reason to take notice and be aware of you. A dog who is alert and aware is far easier to guide into set behaviour patterns.

Deidore Matthews uses a tug-a-knot to switch on her little Sheltie

Motivation

A **Happy Dog** means a **Happy Handler** and *eventually* a **Happy Winner.**

Heather Woodford and Obedience Champion Kirkelly of Stillash (Kelly) after winning the Obedience PRO Dog of the Year 1993 with top judge Kaye Faires

31

Rewards

We all work for something, very few are fortunate enough to work purely for the love of it. Even if we enjoy our work the fact that it becomes a necessity for our survival can turn it into a chore, and the rewards have to be sufficient for us to want to carry on. If the rewards are not readily forthcoming we begin to turn off and are less likely to respond enthusiastically to the task ahead. Good employers recognise this fact and in order to get the best results from their investment, make sure wherever possible, that their employees are rewarded sufficiently to make them want to give it their best shot. Likewise dogs need a reward to make it all worthwhile. The section on *motivation* deals with this in detail.

Reward for a dog can come in many guises, but the important thing to remember is that the dog must realise why he is receiving the reward, if it is to be of any use to your training programme.

The most common rewards are often given without thinking; a kindly word, a soothing voice, a pat on the head, or just a smile. Given at the correct time in association with a correct action or during a training exercise, these can mean just as much to a dog as a bonus in your pay packet does to you.

When teaching your dog to do more complicated and less natural exercises you may need some form of reward which is a little more positive, and can stimulate your dog's natural instincts. A titbit is fine but care must be taken in the administration. The dog must always think that there is another tasty morsel where the last one came from, (even if you've run out!). You must learn to never give so many titbits that the dog is full or bored. You need to become accustomed to reading your dog and giving just enough to leave the dog *'wanting'*. The best way to gauge this is by watching the dog, or by watching someone else with their dog. If the dog walks away or looses interest then the reward has been over done, or is not stimulating enough. It's rather like working in a chocolate factory, (even if you are a choc-o-holic!). At first you can't get enough, but after a while it becomes very boring if not a bit sickly. *(See Motivation)*.

The amusement arcades have rewards all sewn up, they know exactly how to programme the machines for minimum pay out and maximum profit. The game machine has that uncanny knack of paying out a little just as you were about to walk away, and you are stimulated by the reward to stay a little longer to see what else will come your way. Reward training works on the same basis, learn when to give and when to withhold. It takes practice but once perfected it will be an invaluable tool to your training programme.

Using Toys

Toys are by far the best reward because they can always be there, never consumed totally and carried in your pocket and produced at just the right time. A toy to your dog can be a ball or pull, a rope knot, a squeaky toy, or simply a piece of rag, an old sock or piece of carpet. Whatever you use, make sure that it is safe, and of a size that can easily fit into your pocket, and be carried wherever you go with your dog. *(See Toys)*.

Some people have trouble with the dog not wanting to play with a toy, this can be turned around and the dog can be taught to enjoy a game with you and your toy. *(See The Want, and Play training)*.

All rewards must be given, if they are to be of any significance, at precisely the correct time, i.e. in conjunction with the act that you are trying to perfect.*(See timing)* Rewards can be carried as an inducement which will help you to link segments or sections of exercises together, *(see linking)*. Reward can be given to your dog not only when you are teaching something specific but whenever he is displaying good behaviour. As I sit and write with my dog at my feet, I look down and smile and gently praise him as he lies there, and repeat my key word of 'Settle'. I have taught my dog to understand that this means, 'Lie down and keep quiet whilst I am busy'. He slowly thumps his tail on the floor, and is happy and confident, reassured that what he is doing is pleasurable, I am pleased, and all is well. He lays his head back down and drifts off into a twitching doggy sleep chasing sheep in his dreams I guess! So just a small reward given at the right time in a way that the dog can understand helps to keep him happy and contented and makes your life easier.

To keep your dog interested rewards should be varied, but remember if you want a calm quiet response then your reward should be soothing. If you want a lively exuberant response then the reward should be more stimulating.

Ronnie Jones uses her tug toy to reward and stimulate her Great Dane

Play Training

The best way in my view to train a dog is through play. Children learn through play, and it has been seen in cases where children are deprived of play, that they develop all manner of extreme, compulsive, and unnatural behaviour patterns. Play training helps tremendously with motivation, it gives the dog the *'want'* to please and work for you.

Play is a primary motivation. Predatory animals like dogs learn through play, they learn to hunt by perfecting their motor skills and practising their pounce, grab, stalk, tug, etc., which of course is their means to survival. In the wild this would be done with their siblings, dogs are best compared to juvenile wolves, and so play remains an integral part of their lives that we can capitalise on.

Dogs that won't play

Sometimes dogs seem to lack the ability to play, possibly because of the way they have been brought up. Often this is coupled with a placid temperament. Most of these animals can be taught to play even though it may take a long time. They can be motivated into enjoying a game with you. If your dog is one of these unenthusiastic individuals, then close attention to the following training programme will point you in the right direction:

Firstly, pick up all of your dogs toys, balls, chews, etc. this may seem harsh but you and your dog will benefit eventually. Observe your dog's behaviour pattern for a few days and determine when he is at his most exuberant. In some dogs this may be difficult to detect, watch carefully. During this time, ignore your dog as much as possible. Don't make a fuss of him attend only to his needs and ignore his demands. .But for feeding, watering and attending to his bodily functions, pretend that he doesn't exist for a day or two. Again this seems hard but you will reap the rewards in the long run.

When you have identified the time when the dog is most exuberant, (this may be before feeding time, or when you are about to go for a walk), take a tug toy or ball *(see toys),* and start playing with it yourself. Do not at this stage invite the dog to join in, just play by yourself with the toy. If the dog try's to join in then great, allow him to for a few moments only, (don't wait for him to grow bored). Then put away the toy and resume ignoring the dog. Follow the sequence as many times a day as you have detected excitement. Don't try to get the dog to join in, but allow him to if he shows an interest, just have a short game and stop while the dog is still keen. This procedure works particularly well when the dog is hungry as this heightens his excitement and anticipation. Always remember to put the toy away out of the dog's reach. He is only going to be allowed to play if he plays with you, ignore the dog the rest of the time.

Once the dog has shown some interest and you have created a desire in him to join in, (this can take a while with older or more blasé dogs), the toy can then be left in sight, yet still out of reach. This heightens the anticipation of play as the dog can see the toy, but cannot get it until you arrive to have a game. Gradually the dog will want to play, but this method only works, if you refrain from pushing the dog into play, let him acquire *'want'*. Carry on keeping other contact to a minimum until you are confident that your dog will play on the production of his toy.

To 'wean' the dog onto other toys the procedure can be repeated, although it shouldn't take as long the second or third time around.
You can start to incorporate the playing into training, but very short sessions to start with.

This method also works exceptionally well with dogs who are possessive over their toys or will play only with the toy but not with you. If you have more than one dog, until you have mastered the play do not allow the dog which you are training to play with the other dogs as he will be gaining all his enjoyment from them, and is unlikely to see any point in playing with you. It may seem hard but if you want your dog to play with you it is worth persevering - once your dog is fully conditioned he can then gradually be allowed to play with the others but make sure that you always remain favourite - and if necessary repeat the procedure every so often. Do not loose faith, it can take a while but it does work.

How to use it!

Play, particularly when it is incorporating a toy, can be used in all sorts of ways during training to aid motivation *(see motivation)*. It can be used as an immediate reward for carrying out a task, or as an inducement to react to your command. It

Keen, alert Piper is trained by Ann Munks using his lead as motivator

can be used as an incentive to heighten enthusiasm, and brought in at any time during an exercise to motivate the dog. It can also be used to distract the dog from things that you don't want him to do.

Avoid over using the toy to start with. If your dog has not been good at playing in the past, you don't want to bore him, and end up back at square one *(see motivation)*. Likewise with an over excitable dog too much of the toy will prevent him from concentrating on the task ahead - watch your dog and learn from his reactions. Don't be afraid to watch a training exercise go wrong, because by observing carefully you are able to put things right much more quickly and efficiently without distress and confusion being loaded onto the dog. It is far better to isolate a problem by watching and reacting correctly than to use a hit and miss approach.

Many dogs are happy to play with the handler alone, and do not need a toy to motivate them. When bonding with a new puppy - it is always best to aim to teach him to play with yourself as well as a toy - to have a rough and tumble, to chase after your fingers, as well as having a tug of war with a handkerchief, the lead, or a toy that will always be available. Make sure that you always have your motivation tools to hand, they must never run out, get lost or disappear. This gives you a great advantage at times when quick reactions are needed.

Training, through play, is the most satisfactory and pleasurable way of training available. It brings pleasure to the dog, to the handler, and to all who witness it.

Toys and play can be used as the motivator to link exercises or part of exercise together and so produce a stylish, accurate and highly motivated performance. *(See linking)*.

Timing of course plays a big part in the ability to use play correctly. Playing at the wrong time can be distracting and counter productive. For instance when teaching the stay exercise we need the dog to be fairly calm, jumping him around with a toy is not going to create this effect. Depending on the dog's character however, you may use your toy as a motivator to give confidence. Your play toy and your play attitude should become your life line and bond with your dog. If he shows confusion or apprehension at any time you can always pull out your 'Ace card' the toy, and lighten things up!

Teaching the Large Dog

Large often means slower, or more graceful both in body and maturity, at least in comparison to the Border Collie. But the larger dog can be taught to move flexibly and quickly if you build up both his mind and his body tone. There is nothing more graceful or mouth-watering to watch than a large dog working attentively and with style. I use toys and play to build up physical dexterity. Large dogs make a terrific dancing partner, and a little and often gentle hind leg dancing can build up the muscles. Obviously care must be taken in the growth and development stages of the dog, and time must be allowed for the bones, muscles and particularly hips to reach maturity. When the dog is mature physically a little jumping, weaving and swimming, together with games which make erratic or unpredictable movements will strengthen and help the dog to improve mental and physical dexterity. The use of toys which bounce in unpredictable directions will do wonders for the dog's co-ordination and help to make exercise fun as well as productive.

In general people tend to make excuses for larger dogs saying they are too big to be able to perform some of the exercises. This is true in some cases but with general obedience exercises there is normally a way around the problem. Straight forward heel work doesn't normally present a problem, but sometimes intricate or repeated turns can cause anguish, especially left turns. Often this is because the natural heel position of the dog is too far forward, and when the handler attempts to turn her left leg the dog is already too far forward to achieve a neat turn. This results in the dog's position becoming erratic, surging, dipping, or the dog simply waits for the handler to turn and then rejoins the heel position.

It is imperative that you work on keeping the dog's shoulders level with your leg and not forward of you at any time during heel work. This position might feel a little too far back if you are used to having the dog powering forward. Ask someone to watch and tell you if it looks right, remember the rules, the dog's shoulder should be level with your leg. Then, when you have perfected the correct heel position, you will find that you are able to introduce the correct footwork, and so the turn can be performed well.

There have been many examples of large or heavy dogs doing well in competitive obedience. Even if they do not possess the speed in a tight space that the more agile dog can produce, they should, never the less work at a good, natural pace and will not be marked down by a fair judge. Obviously if you are content to let your dog amble around and do not motivate him sufficiently, then you expect to be marked accordingly. The dog should be able to move at a speed, where appropriate, that would be natural if he were playing or self motivated.

Large Dogs

As with any breed that is not genetically programmed to be single minded, it is best not to repeat exercises over and over. Keep your programme varied and your motivation high. Larger dogs need to build up stamina and will take longer to do this than a breed built for endurance like a Collie. So take your time and be patient.

In Britain at the present time, German Shepherds are second only in popularity for obedience to the Working Sheepdog or Border Collie. They are so varied in type and workability that is quite difficult to assess the dog until it has started to mature a little. Some breed lines produce more of a working type than others, and it is worth watching progeny and looking at the family tree if you are thinking of purchasing one, although with the best research in the world nothing is guaranteed. The environment in which the dog is brought up, and the way he is handled and moulded will have a lot to do with the eventual outcome. It is up to you to bring out the best attributes and not to dwell on comparisons with other dogs.

Other large breeds tend to be less popular for one reason or another, but we do have in Britain a smattering of Rottwiellers, Dobermanns, and the odd Standard Poodle, Wolfhound, Great Dane, Newfoundland, Leonberger and others. Abroad it is nice to see many larger breeds working to a very high standard.

If you own and would like to train or retrain a large breed, you will find the methods described in this book quite suitable, they have all been tried and tested on a variety of breeds. You must encourage enjoyment and avoid too much repetition. Give your dog time to mature and develop, just learn to go with the flow. Your dog may learn more quickly than you think, but the second you see confusion stop and re-evaluate your actions. Use obstacles to help you to guide the dog into the correct position. Sometimes it is near on impossible to reach the end of your large dog in order to correctly position his angled bottom! Use a wall to help you.

Use your common sense to make life easier, there is not just *one* way to train a dog. As long as

● *Few obedience dogs are as big as Ronnie Jones'
Great Dane, Helmalake Tudor Minstrel*

38

what you do is kind, well thought out and will not worry the dog then success should come your way.

If you are particularly interested in working a larger breed then it is a good idea to compare a few breed lines, even within your chosen breed. Choose the lines that carry the more extrovert, lively types. Look at back ground, not just the parents but the grandparents and so on. When you have finally got to the stage where you are choosing your pup from the litter, you should look for the most playful, and more importantly, voice and touch sensitive pup. The most dominant pup will not be every one's cup of tea, although in the right hands a dominant dog will make a good working dog. If you are not 100% sure of yourself they are better left to someone else. Remember a dominant dog that becomes aggressive hurts more when its big! Some dogs, even within a breed or litter will have more of the attributes suitable to workability than others, spend as much time as is possible watching the pups both with your intrusion and when left to interact with their siblings, look for the pup that responds well to people.

Heavy dogs like Willow (the author's Leonberger), must be trained with reward and motivation to gain enthusiastic precision, it is virtually impossible to manipulate the dog physically due to its size weight.

39

Small Dogs

Working with small dogs can be fun, but if you are not very careful, back breaking, especially for tall people. Generally small neat handlers make the best small dog workers, but having said that there are, of course always the exceptions.

The same principle can be applied in working small dogs as with large dogs. Methods have to be adjusted and the environment can be used to help. Upright handling is very important as it is even more obvious when the smaller dog has to adjust its position to work to the handler. Some exercises like the close position, the watch, sit, down and stand etc. can be taught with the handler kneeling on the floor or the dog on a table. If using a table, make sure that it is very stable and not inclined to shake or wobble. The surface should be non slip, carpet is ideal.

All the techniques in this book are designed for all breeds, although some of them may need to be scaled down, or involve shorter distances to start with for the smaller dog. Use your own common sense and read your dog's reactions.

Footwork must be extra neat using smaller steps and it will probably be necessary to adjust your stride in order for the smaller dog to keep a consistent rhythm in heel work. Learn to have a gliding gait placing one foot in front of the other keeping your knees as close together as possible. A style which helps all sizes of dog to work neatly, but of utmost importance with smaller dogs because every inch counts. They have less body mass to cover minor inaccuracies, and so you must learn to be super controlled.

Small dogs can play just as tough as larger breeds just like this corgi.

Close fitting trousers are a must so that they do not flap in the dog's face. Your lead should be carefully chosen with two most important considerations in mind. For training a light lead with a dainty clip that doesn't hit the dog. In the ring, where a lead is needed, it may be necessary to use a slightly heavier lead, because the wind can catch a light one and knock it into the dog's face during lead ring work. A cord or fine rope lead is better than a flat one because there is less surface area to catch the wind. For a collar it is not necessary to use anything more than a soft leather or fabric buckled type, comfortably fitted.

Smaller dogs can be just as tough in their own way as larger dogs when it comes to fun and games, don't be afraid of playing tug and having a rough and tumble. Follow all of the pointers in the sections on *play training, motivation* etc. to develop an attentive, happy working dog.

Don't be too repetitive, only the most obsessive of dogs can thrive on training based on the principle of doing it over and over again until it is right, for every time that it comes right there may have been twenty getting it wrong. Which one is the dog to choose next time? The easiest one no doubt, but I wonder if it will be what you want!. Be inventive and imaginative, think clearly before you begin to teach the dog and be sure of what you are doing. If you go wrong don't worry, simply smile and start again. If the dog goes wrong the same applies, start again and help him all of the way so that he can't go wrong again. Reward him when he is correct, and during the time that he is performing the stages of what you are trying to achieve.

Some dogs can be particularly sensitive or gentle in their actions, and you should not try to alter the dog's temperament, but you can develop the animal and help him to enjoy a more outgoing life style and attitude to competition work. Do this by developing the play skills, and use distraction training to help the dog to accept unusual or difficult situations.

Handlers often make the mistake of over protecting smaller dogs, if you have done this then you will need to make a super human effort in teaching your dog more on the social aspects of life, my first book , *'Everybody Can Train Their Own Dog' (TFH)* will help you with this side of things.

If you have just acquired your dog, don't make social training mistakes. Your dog has no concept of size in the same way that we have, and if allowed to mix with friendly dogs of all sizes he will learn to accept them all. Avoid situations that will overwhelm your dog and take things from a distance when necessary. It is often a natural reaction of the small dog owner to pick up the dog when the situation becomes a little too much, try to avoid doing this, let him stand on his own four feet, however small they might be.

Smaller, gentler breeds like Miniature Poodles, Shetland Sheep dogs, Cavaliers, Papilions and the like have plenty of spirit, normally very bidable and make excellent dogs for those new to the sport, children or those not wanting anything to powerful. Corgis and Jack Russels also make a popular choice but can be a little more powerful, both in mind and body.

The most important factors to be considered when training and working with your small dog, is to keep it fun, interesting, keep your handling neat and controlled and don't bore the poor dog's socks off!

Teaching sensitive dogs

Sensitive dogs need an especially caring hand. You must be particularly careful not to become confusing in your approach to teaching and indeed to every day life. It is very easy to go wrong with any dog but with a sensitive dog it can be harder to deal with and put right.

Your attitude to the dog will have much bearing on the outcome. You must be positive, friendly and outgoing without being over the top. The dog must see you in control of situations so that he can gain confidence from you. Many outwardly spirited dogs are quite sensitive underneath, and once you are able to observe and identify this these dogs are a pleasure to work with.

Sensitivity is a human characteristic and in dogs normally the behaviour would be identified with a more specific name, submissiveness may perhaps be the category that they fit into, although not all sensitive dogs are particularly submissive. Sometimes they are socially insecure, fearful of the unknown, lacking in confidence, etc. A little bit of sensitivity can be a positive

Some dogs need extra special handling and a very kind and patient attitude in order to get the best results.

asset in the training game, making the dog a very biddable workmate. Where sensitivity is a problem, it is useful to try to understand what makes your dog sensitive, what situations trigger it off and then build on confidence particularly in those situations, using common bonds. Being sensitive is often the label given to a dog who is confused and so withdraws, unwrap the confusion and the dog is more confident and ultimately becomes outgoing.

42

Sensitive dogs

Of course every dog is different in character even within the same litter of pups there can be terrific swings in temperament which develop even before they go to their new homes. Sometimes it is extremely difficult to get the type of attitude that you want because even with the best training in the world many of the behavioural idiosyncrasies are genetically programmed or learnt from the mother and siblings. Therefore it is best to accept your dog for what he is and build on all of the good things. Instil confidence as you go, and use the dog's natural behaviour to your advantage. Choose situations where the dog is naturally confident and build bonds that the dog can identify with to link you across to more difficult areas.

A sensitive dog should be a pleasure for the less abrasive handler to train. You should work through things as a team. Build on confidence, train methodically and yet with variation. With careful planning on your part you should make a great partnership.

Lynn Cartwright's Ellie soon learnt to have fun in a caring and relaxed environment at summer camp

Teaching the keen dog

Define keen; OTT (over the top), hyper active, nutty, head strong, head in the clouds, head banger! All terms that people use to describe dogs which are more lively than the average. The keen dog is a super tool to work with, but generally the handler's biggest crime is that they try to suppress the keenness instead of using it, or allow the dog to become out of hand for fear of losing the keenness.

You must learn to channel the energy into what you are trying to achieve. Many dogs will become obsessive, particularly over toys or retrieve articles. They will seem to be uncontrollable in the presence of one of these items. The chapter on *eliminating* the *aids* will help you to learn how to use those toys to your advantage and to maintain control at the same time. Sometimes you will need to hide the toy behind your back or in your pocket until you get the dog's concentration on the matter in hand. Then quickly bring out the toy to use as reward for correct behaviour which may be purely good concentration. Use the exercises that you teach the dog, not as a threat but as a part of the game.

Rookie (OB CH Charouska Kris Moss) is one of the keenest dogs in obedience today. Janet Matthews handles him with a calm and fair attitude, always rewarding good behaviour, and quietly showing him what is required.

Keen dogs especially should be taught that the words *'Good boy',* mean that you are pleased. *(See Rewards)* The keen dog can then be rewarded without even a toy or titbit being brought out, but make sure that you have built a good bond with your keen dog, and that he trusts you.

44

Keen Dogs

Dogs, like humans, naturally try to avoid things which are not pleasurable and will attempt to go on to those things which they can enjoy. So it is important to accustom yourself to making all sections of an exercise part of the whole, an exciting and pleasant experience, instead of addressing threat to the static parts and allowing the dog freedom to be over keen in other parts.

The retrieve is once again a good example to use. Handlers who fear that they will lose control will yell and threaten when attempting to keep the dog at heel. This makes the chase of the retrieve article all the more attractive to the dog! Not only is the out run and grab of the article fun, but it is release from your nagging! Use your tools, your toy or your retrieve article as an incentive to perform the control parts of the exercise. The principles are explained in the section which deals with teaching the retrieve. This principle will work in all aspects of training your dog.

The dog's behaviour is shaped into what you want with the incentive as reward. The secret is learning when to reward and when to withhold, when to keep the article out of sight and when to have it in full view and or in joint possession of you and the dog. Develop the dog's attitude to be just as obsessive over all parts of the exercise as he may be over the chasing or fast movement sections. Use one of the objects of his obsession as reward and motivation, but choose carefully, if something is just too desirable for words, put it away and use something else until you have better control.

Approach the exercises in a calm and pleasant manner, do not become hyped up yourself. The dog needs a sound base on which to focus. With patient handling he will learn when to use his energy. The *'Watch'* exercise will be of particular use to you, much time and effort should be afforded to teaching this in a calm, structured, pleasant manner.

The sections on *Timing* and *Motivation* will help you and in the *Techniques* section you will see that I have addressed the variables of character in teaching each exercise.

Do not to suppress the spirit - use it!

Teaching the hard dog

What is a hard dog?

'Hard' **is a term** we hear banded regularly, normally accompanied by a callous statement regarding beating the hell out of the dog and it making no difference! This to me shows total misunderstanding of dogs. Remember the genetically programmed instinct of all dogs, is to survive and to reproduce. They like humans, can not alter this. Unlike us they do not have the mental capacity to ignore these needs unless we give them alternatives, based on those needs, on which they can focus their energies. The term *'hard'* when it is analysed, probably means not very sensitive and sometimes dominant, although I know most people will be able to come up with an exception. There are always grey areas and terms like hard, sensitive, etc. are very broad bands, and after all humanism's.

With a dog which you feel fits this category you will find it easier to deal with if you give yourself chance to sit back and observe his behaviour. Identify what situations trigger the sort of drive that you find it difficult to deal with. Identify the times when the animal is easier and more biddable and use that knowledge to gain success by building tour training patterns on the easy times. Teach the dog that it is fun to be with you and to respond to you and keep friendly control at that point. The more you take control of his life, the more the dog will accept you in control, and so without a battle, you begin to reap the benefits. By the phrase taking control, I don't mean yanking him off his feet on a check chain, beating him with a newspaper or worse! All that is meant is that the dog becomes accustomed to, and enjoys **you** controlling things instead of **him.**

For most handlers the problem creeps up on them as the animal matures. As puppies the dogs are reasonably pliable if they are guided in the right direction, and any signs of problems are often passed off as 'cute'. But, as time goes by the dog develops, handling is misguided, tempers fray and life becomes more difficult. Finding the right type of motivation, using the dog's natural behaviours to your advantage, and ignoring times when it is hard to get through will start to see success. Read the chapters on *motivation, reward and play training* to help you to develop the dog's character into a more acceptable working medium.

Teaching the old dog new tricks

Whether you are taking on the training and care of an older dog from someone else, or you have decided that you wish to retrain your own older dog, you must learn to edge your way carefully watching for confusion in your dog and not mistaking confusion for disobedience.

Dogs have two main motivators, self preservation and self duplication, i.e. food and sex! Most correctly fed dogs find titbits very welcome, and those who are not particularly interested in food extras often turn on to play. Food and play are directly linked because, as with most predatory species, play is the natural way of learning about life and to hunt for food. So the same survival instinct is driving both the need for food and play. This is why these two motivation tools are the best to use in training. *(See the sections on play training, motivation and rewards.)*

To train older dogs you really have to pretend that they are puppies to a certain degree. You need to allow time to build a confidence and a trust bond between you and the animal. At the same time you must maintain control calmly and in a pleasant manner yourself. A dog who is anxious will not be helped by an anxious handler. Do not put yourself into situations where you are not confident that you can control the dog or others around you. Build on your own attitude, confidence, and self control. Approach difficult situations from a distance for instance, if you have difficulty keeping the dog's attention on you in the presence of other dogs or people, do not go right into the middle of them and struggle with the dog. Stand on the out skirts, allow the dog time to take things in and then when he is more settled, and the novelty has worn off start a game. The duration of the game should be for just a few seconds to begin with. Try to instigate the game and end it yourself, so that you maintain control. Forget formal obedience exercises for now, just get that team spirit developing and enjoy your dog. Many is the time that new handlers to my class have been sent way down the field out of the way of the others, not because we want them out of the way, but because it is much easier for the handler to get positive results. Then gradually over a period of time the new handler and dog get closer and closer to the hubbub of things. In only a few sessions they are in the middle of the class playing with the dog. *Now the handler has a tool they can use it!*

Often it is easier taking second hand or rescue dog than it is to re-educate your own, but both have their draw backs. With the second hand dog you are never 100% sure what has happened to the dog, even if in theory you know where they have come from. Often the story is distorted or down right untrue to make the previous owner feel better or more justified in parting with the dog. So you must allow time to assess the dog's character and learn how you can both feel comfortable in all situations. On the other hand you can't be too laid back and allow things to happen that you know in the long run are not going to be acceptable. Careful guidance of the dog with calm control will avoid these problems. Teach ground rules without aggression, don't forget that a dog sees aggression as loss of control. A truly dominant animal never needs to assert more than the odd low key grumble in order to maintain his position. It is not in his interest to fight, he shows his authority in the way that he lives his life to maintain proper control of the dog you must do the same.

With the older dog that you yourself have made mistakes with but now have seen the light and want to put things right, you need to decide on your aims. Decide what you definitely *don't* want, and avoid situations that would spark off that behaviour until you have developed distractive methods to control the dog *(see distraction training)*. Decide on what you definitely *do* want, read carefully and try to absorb information from the concepts section, learn techniques from the technique section which will promote the required behaviour. Do *not* try to *correct* the behaviour or exercises that are wrong as this leads to confusion. Simply start over again once you have a clear understanding of what you want to achieve and how to go about it.

Mary Griffiths and Holly learning how to use play.

Ignore and guide the dog away using distraction training, from anything that you don't want. Putting all of the emphasis and reward on to what you are trying to achieve will make the dog home in to those things, and gradually by extinction the other behaviours will start to fade away.

In our class we had one handler who's dog was besotted with other dog's squeaky toys. She had struggled at shows for months, every time her dog heard a squeak his attention to his handler was gone. Much to her horror I suggested she stopped fighting it and bought him a squeaky of his own. With careful distraction training and following the procedure to hide the incentives we soon taught the dog that whenever he heard a squeaky it could be his own. His attention improved and the handler now actually benefits from outside of the ring squeaks.

Old Dogs New Tricks

Another handler had a six year old Samoyed which had been taught obedience in a very hard handed fashion. The dog did not know how to play with the handler and was totally negative in his approach to obedience. After a short course using play, motivation, timing, and understanding, the dog began to work through choice, and both handler and dog began to enjoy themselves. At the end of the course the handler burst into tears when I asked her why she replied that she was just so overwhelmingly happy with the difference in her dog in just a few short days of positive happy training.

I have had personal experience of both second hand dogs and retraining my own older dogs which I had made my mistakes on ('Yes - non of us are perfect'!) The secret is to admit to your self that even though you are supposed to have the superior intelligence and are supposed to be the teacher you are capable of getting it wrong. If the dog is going wrong then it is *your fault*. If things have gone wrong just laugh and start again.

To sum up. Think clearly and positively before you start, be sure of what you *are* and *are not* trying to achieve. Build a bond. Be patient. Keep control. Admit that you can be wrong. Don't loose sight of your objectives, but most of all **keep it fun.**

Toys

Toys are a very important part of your dog training kit. To achieve the best results with toys as training aids, other toys should not be left available for your dog to play with at will. Remember you are using your toys as a reward and to increase motivation. If you have constant access to almost *anything* it looses it's appeal after a while, as anyone who has ever worked in a chocolate factory will agree! If you feel you need to leave something down for your dog then a safe chew or pacifier would be a better choice, save the exciting toys for the training sessions when you will want to generate all the interest and enthusiasm. Few dogs really need toys left scattered around and indeed this can lead to dominant tendencies in some dogs. *(My book 'Everybody can train their own dog, published by TFH, and the behaviour booklets published by Rainbow Publishing deal with any behavioural problems of this vein).*

If you are carrying out your training programme correctly, your dog will be receiving plenty of mental stimulus and fun from you. Very young puppies perhaps will benefit from a few toys whilst you are out, but you must always make sure that these are completely safe to be left, i.e. the puppy cannot chew and swallow bits of them, make sharp edges, nor can he throw them up in the air and then catch them in his throat. Even with young puppies I prefer to leave only one or two well chosen chew toys, and then produce the exciting 'stuff' when I'm around to control and enter into the game. When I leave or decide the game is over, the toys go with me leaving the dog wanting more, this is the first stage of achieving *'The Want'.(See 'The Want')*

The type of toys that you use are much a case of personal or canine preference. Some dogs will be motivated by anything that moves whilst others will take a little more stimulating.

There have been many toys developed over the past few years, some of them by my husband Michael White, which are specifically made for inducing team play between you and your dog. A game of tug with both you and the dog holding the toy will help you to develop a sense of team spirit, but remember you must always win in the end and the toy must remain yours, if you are to remain pack leader. The dog can be allowed to grasp the toy, but if he is kept on lead during play sessions you will always remain in complete control. If you release the lead the dog can go hurtling where ever he pleases and he is then no longer playing with you but simply playing with the toy. This will not help your team work, you

Toys

must teach your dog, and condition yourself that play and reward are at their most exciting when you are working close together as a team.

Many handlers complain that although their dog will play, he lacks sparkle in his work and often the reason is that all the pleasure of the toy, all the sense of achievement and reward has come to the dog when he has been away from the handler.

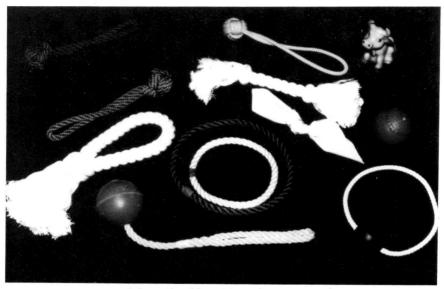

Safe toys if used for training under proper control

So the main things to remember about toys as training aids are:

1) The toys belong to you **not** the dog.

2) They should not be left down for the dog to play with at will, (particularly if you have a problem with the dog not wanting to play with you, or with dominance).

3) The toys should be safe.

4) They should be compact enough to fit into your pocket.

5) The toys should be used with care, learn when to give and when to withhold.

And remember, keep play sessions close to you and maintain full control. Keep your dog on lead. Your reason for using toys is to help make training and working fun with you, not in the next ring, the next field or with another dog!

Equipment

There are some very important items, but after that it depends on how much you are prepared to carry about. Obstacles, bollards, markers, retrieve articles, scent cloths, lots of variation will make training interesting and less repetitive, so start collecting!

The most important items are as follows; a soft leather or fabric collar, fairly broad so that it does not cut into the dog, and can also serve as a useful handle if your dog is off lead. The lead is a case of personal preference. Try to go for something reasonably light, but it must feel comfortable in your hands. Thick braided rope is my favourite, solely because it is so comfortable to handle, it is tough, washable and reasonably cheap. If I decide to use it as a play toy it can easily be replaced when it gets tattered without hurting my piggy bank too much! Around about four feet in length will be sufficient for all exercises, any longer than this and you are not in full control, it takes too long to reel your dog in and you will all to easily lose your momentum, and then the dog may as well be off lead for all the control you have, (or rather don't have).

The most important part of your equipment is your toy or *'want aid'*, this will be your life line, so make sure you choose something that can be easily replaced if you lose it or it gets too battered to use. Rope tugs or quoits are ideal, also tug-a-balls etc. *(see toys).* You can even have your toy incorporated with in your lead. Another very useful training item is a set of poles to make up a practice ring, light plastic ones are fine.

As well as lead, collar and toys, some ring furniture such as bollards or markers will be useful, and perhaps some poles to set up a ring, *(see circuit training).* A dumbbell or course is needed for the retrieve exercise in the competition ring. In Britain one good quality dumb-bell is sufficient, don't be tempted to go for something too large that might slop about in your dog's mouth, better to have it on the small side as long as the sides don't hit his eyes. Whilst we train for the dog to pick up anything we don't want to put any unnecessary problems in his path.

You will need some cloth squares for scent work, preferably include some with weights sewn inside so that you can accustom the dog to picking up weighted cloths similar to the ones he will find in the ring. Scent boards to attach cloths to will be invaluable in your training, preventing the dog from picking up the wrong

Equipment

one, thus training for success. You will need some tongs or thick plastic gloves to handle neutral, decoy cloths or scent articles, and you are just about there.

It will be of benefit to you and the dog if you consider the type of clothes that you wear for training and competing. Trousers are a must for everyone, but these should not be too loose or made of a *noisy* fabric. Pockets in your upper garment will be of great use, because then you are able to hide your want aid out of sight, but it is very easily brought back to motivate the dog.

One most important item is a patient and pleasant attitude, with a willingness to accept the fact that if the dog goes wrong then it is more than likely you the trainer who is at fault rather than the dog!

Techniques

Techniques

TECHNIQUES

Before you start

Before embarking on any of the techniques described in this section you must first consider several points. Most importantly you must ask yourself, 'Do I really understand the concepts? Can I easily recall the importance and apply split second accuracy of timing? Have I formed a true bond with my dog? Does he respond the second I appear and give him motivation, whatever the circumstances? Does my dog truly 'Want' to play and to be with me? Do I really understand how his mind works? Am I prepared to have fun and keep my patience with my dog?'

If you can confidently answer 'Yes' to all of the above then you can now move on to learning the techniques of teaching your dog. If you have any doubts, then it won't hurt, in fact it will be beneficial to go back over any grey areas, make notes as you go through if it helps, and treat your work as if you were studying a subject that you were to be examined on. This may seem a little extreme but, after all, if you are to be entering competitions then you are offering yourself up for scrutiny and you really should know your subject as well as possible.

If you are pleased with the results of a technique that you are already using to teach your dog, then there is no need to change just because the technique described in this book might be different. Most techniques used in teaching for competition today will be effective as long as they are kind and fair to the dog, and used in conjunction with the concepts described in the first section of this book. Don't complicate matters, all techniques should be kept as simple as possible, both for you to be able to implement correctly, and for the dog to understand and learn.

Teach all techniques step by step and make sure that *you* understand what you are trying to achieve at each step, as well as the ultimate goal, *before* you start on the poor dog. Be positive in everything you do and you will get a positive response from your dog. If his response is not what you wanted then stop and check on, and carefully scrutinise what you are doing.

Remember *you* are the teacher, the dog is but the pupil. He can only learn if you show him in a way that he can understand. If the dog goes wrong do **not** chastise, simply start all over again and make sure that *you* get it right this time. Help the dog all of the way and enjoy the learning process together.

REMEMBER - HAPPY DOGS MAKE HAPPY WINNERS!

Voice - Tones and Usage

What you do with your voice is of utmost importance in your dog training. Firstly I will deal with tones. It is important to stay in control of your vocal chords, a change in tone even if your are saying the same word can mean a totally different thing to the dog. Experiment yourself by saying the dog's name in differing tones and watch his reactions. Some handlers even teach exercises such as distance control or sending the dog to heel *(the finish),* just using differing tones of the dog's name as the key words. It is quite acceptable to do this, and the dog will learn to respond very well so long as the handler is consistent.

Voice tone can mean many things to the dog, it can mean pleasure, reward, interest, boredom, fear, or something to be avoided. When using your voice in training you must make sure that the tone which you use to teach the dog is the same tone that you use when you want the dog to perform the task. Many handlers make vital mistakes when transferring the trained exercise to a ring situation. Because of the distance the handler needs the voice to carry, the tone quite naturally changes, sometimes because of nerves or anxiety regarding the dog's, or indeed their own ability to perform under the pressure of a ring situation. Whatever the reason handlers very often do not sound the same as they do in training. This is most confusing for the dog, and often the dog ends up being chastised for his misunderstanding when really the handler was not putting over their wishes in a way that the dog could understand, and therefore the dog should not have been expected to perform correctly.

It is with this in mind that as a handler you must train yourself to use the same tones as those that you intend to use in the ring. To create this is often best to put yourself in a mock up situation without the dog.

Let us take the sendaway as an example of when a keyword is needed at a distance. *'Down',* when the dog is in the correct area at the distance. As a Northerner I personally find it very difficult to push the 'down' word out with any carrying power, therefore I copied my Southern friends and gave the word a more drawn out centre, *'D-a-a-o-wn'.* I found this a more comfortable pronunciation, and was able to push the word out with some power. But everyone is different and you need to experiment, not just in the house but outside in areas that might be like a show ground. You will find that a voice that carries well in 12' x 15' room in the house, might not sound as powerful in a field. Once you have decided on your word and tone usage, and have accustomed yourself to using the same each time until it becomes natural to you, then you can start to teach the dog, using your play training, to associate your voice and tones with the actions that you would like him to perform. Remember, if you have had to re-think some of your pronunciations and tones, then you will have to give the dog every opportunity of getting it right. That means *'Training',* **not** just going through the motions of the exercise, actually show the dog what you want, as if he had never done it before, this way he will learn very quickly, and we will prevent errors from creeping in. This will save lots of time and frustration on the part of both the dog, and you as the handler.

Use of verbal commands

Just about everyone, at the outset of training their dog, introduces the use of far too many verbal commands, sometimes expecting the dog to understand whole sentences, and cluttering their key words with lots of added extras for good measure. It is much easier for the dog if we keep the key words to a bare minimum, it is certainly easier having done this, to eliminate verbal commands ready for the higher classes. The typical heel work vocabulary with the inexperienced handler consists of a variation on the following: 'heel, close, watch, watch me, get in, come on, tight, back, turn, that's good, what have I got, bum in, what's this then, where's your squeaky, good boy, clever, rubbish, Oih!' together with an assortment of noises which I will leave to your imagination - I could go on! An incredible variety and quantity of messages being put over to the dog all really meaning one thing - follow my left leg please. Go along to any beginner/novice ring and listen to the cacophony of verbals. Then, watch out for the experienced handler with their young dog, competing in the same ring. Often their dog will be among the youngest competing in that class, and yet the handler will not be uttering anything like the amount of commands and verbal stimulus.

Normally the dog who does not have to contend with all this 'verbal diarrhoea' will be much more attentive, and find it easier to concentrate with the aid of just a little well timed help from the handler. *(See Timing).*

For those who I can now hear saying that their dog works attentively and they *do* give lots of verbal stimuli, I pose this question, what will your dogs work like after a few attempts in the higher classes without the aid of your voice? Nine times out of ten, when the handler shuts off the noise the dog is confused and less motivated. The handler then becomes frustrated and if we are not very careful loses their temper with the dog into the bargain. Of course the dog then sinks even lower, and I feel that this common fault is one of the major reasons for the high drop out rate of handlers or rejection of dogs after the first two classes. Many handlers come into the sport with non-standard breeds, (as far as obedience is concerned), perhaps this basic problem is a contributory factor as to why so many of them give up and then come back into the sport with the almost compulsory Collie.

If you are recognising yourself at this point please do not feel that you must be one of the drop outs, all is not lost. Because you have recognised the problem you are half way on the road to solving it. As you work through the exercises in the next section of the book, you will see that *one* key word only is necessary to trigger each action, and the dog will learn to follow through the exercise solely on that one key word, with just added encouragement in the early stages or at any time that you feel the dog needs an extra boost of confidence.

The sections on *Understanding the Dog's Mind, Motivation* and *Play Training* will help you to know when, and how intensely to give reward and encouragement, and the sections on triggers and linking will explain how the dog is able to understand how to perform following one key word only, a complicated task.

Routines

To help you as a dog trainer to be consistent and positive, it is important that you have some set ideas or routines to get you and your dog into the swing of things at each training session and before you go into the ring. An Olympic sprinter would not be expected to go straight out on to the track and do a 500 metre sprint without first warming up. Nor would we expect a college graduate to go in for an exam without first doing some revision, no matter how clever he was. So why should we expect our dogs to go straight into a full advanced or even beginner round without some form of warm up session that gets both his mind and body into gear. Now to some, this means marching up and down doing heel work and anything else that might be a particular problem at the time, practising the faults as they go! But for me a set routine of tightening up and warming up exercises, that will not allow faults, but will re-confirm the precision required, with lots of incentive and motivation, has to be a better idea. Obviously with a dog who is just starting to learn the exercise then you can only go as far as you have taught, and then possibly, push on a little further if the dog is confident and happy. But with an older, and for the best part trained, dog you can have quite a comprehensive warming up and training routine. Start from the beginning each time with a little play.

Your training routine, all conducted with the dog on lead, could go something like this:

1) The Want - Play with your dog, get him in *play mode*, and make sure you have the *'Want'*.

2) Attention - Guide your dog into the heel position with the *'Watch'* key word. Get half a second of perfect watch - then play. Build up your time as you did when teaching the exercise, but moving quickly yet progressively on to the next step with each success, praising and playing after each break.

3) Heel work - Guide your dog into the heel position give the *'Watch'* key word, and then *'Close'*, take one step forward with the dog in perfect position, and paying attention to you - then break and play. Just one step of perfect heel work, then start again and the next time go for two. Building like this keeping everything

61

Routines

fun and keeping up the want all of the time. The next time go for three steps of perfection, then four and so on but not going further than the dog is capable of maintaining full attention and the *'Want'*. If at any time he looses concentration, you are going on to far. Start again and set your sights a little lower.

4) Turns - Go through all of your training techniques for turns, the present, the finish starting by guiding the dog at a leads length, and then gradually closing in.

5) Retrieve - starting with the hold, and then moving on through the progression of segments, don't miss anything and keep up the momentum of motivation.

6) Sendaway - start with the instant down close to you on lead of course, controlled and using your *'Want'* aids to keep up the excitement. Having previously set up an area to send your dog place his toy to the back of the area and then from a few feet away send him and follow up putting him in the down, and then allow him his toy. Build up your distance, but only going as far as the dog is ultra-confident, and maintain the 'want'.

7) Scent - Take a cloth or similar article, allow the dog to hold as in the first stage of retrieve. Next take a few steps of heel work and drop the cloth and let the dog search back to find it. Next move to a different area and do the search back with some other immovable objects around, improvise if you are out in a field by using stones, etc.

8) Distance Control - Go through each position in a fun manner playing between every one, and going through the training procedure in quick progression to your best standard but without doing the finished article as if in the ring.

9) Stays - place your dog in each of the positions in turn, going through the training procedure.

10) Linking - Link some parts of exercises together keeping the flow going all of the time.

11) Circuit training - keep the dog's interest high by being varied in your routines

Remember allow your dog time to do some 'doggy things' release him and let him sniff around and relax if he wants to. Call him to you only when you are sure of getting a perfect and positive response. His reaction to you must be positive 100%

in the ring therefore, outside of the ring, we must learn how to engineer the situation if necessary to maintain a positive response. If when your dog is released he turns a 'deaf ear' then you must learn how to be the most interesting thing around. (Turn to the section on *distraction training* if you have any problems.)

Remember in all things you must make the decisions, or at least the dog must think you did!

Linking

It is important to teach your self to link things together and to look at things from a dog's point of view. By breaking exercises into segments for teaching we are making sure that the dog understands every part of the set piece. But then, if the exercises are to be performed with enthusiasm and to maintain *'The Want'*. The dog needs to see each section of an exercise as a catalyst leading to the conditioned response of. the next thing that we need if we are to get good results in the ring. The ability to link without causing anticipation is the sign of a good dog trainer. Toys, play, and the techniques that we have dealt with to achieve 'The Want', will help you to learn how to link.

Keeping the enthusiasm bubbling, and the dog's full attention on you, will help to make sure that the dog puts things together how you want him to. If you do not maintain full attention then he will miss the next signal, and therefore the link. If you wish to keep your dog's full attention you must learn to give him yours. This is often difficult if you are receiving instruction, but if you watch the best handlers, they never ignore their dog at the end of an exercise. Even if they are demonstrating with a dog they will give him his release command before turning to the audience. Therefore the dog learns that unless told to finish, there is always something interesting about to happen, and he is motivated to keep his attention on the handler. If you are distracted it is not unreasonable to expect the dog to be distracted to. The more this is allowed to happen the less likely you are able to maintain a link between exercises or even segments of exercises.

As your dog progresses and becomes confident in what you are trying to achieve, it is important to link exercises together as you will be expected to in the ring, often going from one to another, but remembering to keep up the *'Want'* with a toy, play, titbit or praise. To give you an example try breaking in the middle of some heel work and have a good play session, then using your *'Want'* aids to go back into heel work for a few yards and link into retrieve, after which play again. This teaches the dog that you don't always finish something in the same place every time, and that there is always some more fun to come.

Linking is also about joining parts of exercises, and incorporating static basic routines into on the move action. For instance take a static taught left turn and put it into fluid heel work in such away that the dog can understand, then execute the turn with precision, and confidence. This again can be taught with your *'want'* aids, guiding and linking each part together, over-

Linking

emphasising moves to make it obvious to the dog. *(See Heel Work).* Always leaving the dog yearning for more, not switched off or lethargic with boredom or confusion.

The Watch

Before you start - you must have achieved 'The Want'.

The watch is probably the most important single exercise you will ever teach your dog. Before starting this or any other exercise, you should first of all establish the 'Want'. If your dog does not want to be with you, to work with you as a team, nor have you formed a bond, then you will have an uphill struggle and probably never reach the heights that you wish to attain.

What do we want from the dog when we say *'Watch'?*

Basically we are saying 'Pay attention to me whatever you are doing, look and listen ready for your next command or signal'. A lot for a dog to take in from one single command. But with patient guidance and a lot of love and play, this can be achieved. Obviously some dogs and handlers will find it easier than others.

Using everything you have learnt in the concepts section, the basic technique is as follows: The key word I use is *'Watch',* but if you know that you have already frightened your dog with this word then change to another to make it easier for you to retrain the dog as the *new you*. Choose your word carefully so that it can not be confused with any others that you use.

Teaching the watch is a good *'hearth rug'* exercise, i.e. you can do it any time that you and the dog are together preferably, to start with at least, it should be done with no distractions. When the dog becomes competent and confident, distractions will be added and worked against. You can start this exercise at any age, as long as the dog is happy and confident with you.

Step one - As with all teaching, start

The Watch

off with a game and a cuddle, a titbit or a toy to get the dog switched on to you. Go down to the dog's level, i.e. on the floor with a smaller dog or puppy, (sitting on a chair, or standing with a bigger dog). Talk to him in excited tones, stimulate him with his toy or titbit. Hold the motivator up towards your face, as soon as you have eye contact, say the key word *'Watch'*, immediately reward with your incentive, then break the exercise giving your release command, *'That'll do'*. Keep up the momentum and the *'want'* by playing.

Repeat the procedure when you are sure that you have the *'want'*. The initial eye contact need only be for a fraction of a second, the object is to get it right and give immediate praise so that the dog knows that he has done a correct action, and that you are pleased. If you try to hold the eye contact too long the dog has the option, and it becomes increasingly tempting for him to look away, then you are teaching nothing. Eye contact could be construed by the dog as a dominant stare, and he will have no option but to look away if he feels dominated by you. (If it were any other way you would have problems). So make sure that *your eyes* show friendship and fun, never threat. It is not necessary for the dog to look at you eye to eye, the word *'Watch'* could come to mean watch my hand, or simply watch my body stance. The dog will be reading all of these signs, and acting on his learnt responses to them. He picks up far more from your body than he does from words. So, as long as he looks at you in connection with that word then we are going in the right direction.

Remember your aim, that is to teach the dog to look at you and pay full attention when he hears the key word *'watch'*. Fractions of seconds of perfection are worth months of corrective training.

Step two - Once the dog is happy to watch you for a fraction then you can progress to half a second. If your timing is correct and you are truly praising the dog at the correct time, he can then associate your praise and play with the action. Analyse yourself and be sure that the dog is being praised at the exact time that he responding correctly. If his eyes are looking elsewhere then you are either going on to quickly, he is confused or you are not portraying the correct attitude, and the dog may feel dominated.

Step three - Once the dog is happily watching in the play sessions you can progress to having the dog sit by your side. Start off at dog level, kneel on the floor or sit sideways on a low chair if you have a small dog. Place the dog in the sit position by your side, guide his face up to look at you, stroke the velvety bit of the dog's nose and calmly teach him that it is a pleasant and soothing place to be as well as a fun place. Then, when the dog is watching put in the *'watch'* key word, release and play. Spend time at this and the above stage, repeating several times at each play or bonding session, or any time you feel like it, in the house or garden.

Step four - When you are sure the dog knows what you mean when you say watch, you can start to introduce some distractions. Start off with something not too attractive, like a person sitting quietly, or a quiet but new environment.

Step five - Once the dog is coping with all of the above you can introduce your own more realistic distractions, one at time of course. Drop the lead, sneeze, have someone speak, work against another dog, another handler training, etc. Be fair to the dog tell him what you want, don't try to catch him out all the time. That is not what it is all about. You are teaching and should make the atmosphere stable and enjoyable, not threatening.

Step six - Teach the dog to watch, not just in the heel position, but when left in the sit, the stand, and the down. Put him in the sit, tell him *'Sit, Watch'*. Gently leave him to a lead's length, repeating both words. Use your toy/titbit to keep his attention. Go back still talking, and gently position yourself back in the heel position. Praise him, reward and release. Repeat for the other positions. This will be a useful exercise for DC, Recalls etc.

Step seven - Repeat any and all of the above, anytime, anywhere, to continually remind the dog what is required when he hears the key word *'Watch'*.

Temperament test

Before you start - Your dog should be confident in you, his lead and collar. He should have developed the 'Want'. Although the finished exercise is to be done in the stand, it does not matter when you first start training, which position the dog is in, it is more important to teach him to enjoy being stroked by others.

The use of your *'want'* aid or titbits will be of paramount importance in teaching this test. The dog needs to associate people approaching him with something pleasant but on the other hand it is not good policy to allow the dog to jump all over the prospective judge. The exercise is not a stand stay, but the dog should learn to stay in the stand position, preferably with all four feet on the ground, and be stroked by anyone.

Step one - Teach the dog to enjoy being stroked by you, whilst he is in the stand position at your side, *(see teaching the stand in the stays section)*. If you cannot manage the stand with any precision yet don't worry, the dog can still do the rest. Use a titbit or his toy in front of his nose to focus his attention.

Step two - The dog now must learn that not everyone will have a sensible approach and sometimes will make fast or sudden movements, or have things (like clipboards) in their hands. Have the dog in the stand and hold a titbit in your right hand, allow the dog to nibble at your fingers, attempting to get at the titbit, bring your left hand a little faster than normal around to stroke the dog, and at the point where you come into contact with the dog's back, and start to stroke release the titbit. Your timing needs to be good, do not release the titbit and allow the dog to jump away as your hand approaches, he must associate the hand with reward.

Step three - When the dog is confident in step two you can increase the speed that your hand approaches the dog, and also the intensity, some judges will be quite rough albeit unintentional. Don't put too much emphasis on the dog staying in the stand position, it is more important that he is not worried by the experience.

Step four - Once the dog is happy and confident with all of the above you can enlist the help of a friend to act as the first introduction to the dog. Instruct them on how to approach your dog, i.e. they should keep their body upright, and to start with simply walk past the dog, whilst you keep his attention on you with a treat. You can then gradually work through the stages building up, making sure that the dog is confident before moving on.

Step five - Use many friends and associates to follow the steps as above. Make sure that they all build up the dog's confidence before being too presumptuous. Soon you will find that the dog is blasé to any situations like these, and if a judge is clumsy in their approach it will not cause you problems for the future.

Trouble shooting

If your dog does have a bad experience in the ring then to start at step one of this section will help enormously, but you must take extra care to go slowly through the stages making sure that the dog's confidence builds all the time. Careful choice of friends to help is also important. Don't opt straight away for the type, sex or size of person that frightened the dog before, these can be carefully and gently introduced much later when the dog has been flooded with good occurrences. Using a friend the dog prefers as a block, the more frightening person can start behind them and walk by as inconspicuously as possible, so that the dog hardly notices.

It may be beneficial to change your key word for stand in the temperament test so that you eliminate any bad associations with your word usage.

Preparing for the Ring

Make sure that the dog is aware of any possible links between exercises, i.e. he must be able to follow from any of the other tests. In the Novice class the temperament test always precedes heel on lead and in the A class it precedes heel free so it is easy to teach a link out. *(See Linking)*

Heel Work

Heel work should not just purely be broken down into simply teaching turns, teaching the heel position, and then working on the move. Although this is a basis, it is much more complex if you want the top results. For instance once the turns are taught at the static position many handlers then assume that the dog will be competent enough to automatically put things together in the ring, or even in training. It must be remembered at all times that the dog is not a mind reader (although he often appears to be one step ahead of his handler!), he needs to be taught and reminded all of the time about the sort of precision that you require. Reminding him does not mean going through the motions of a pattern of heel work at each training session! Reminding him means going through the basic steps, breaking down each exercise as you did when you initially taught him.

This basic step by step training should

Ready for Heel work, notice the expression on Sheila Farris' face full of enthusiasm, ensuring that Flash is confident in her

be done at each training session and where possible on the show ground before entering the competition. *(See Routines).* Of course you should always be striving to maintain *'the want'* and any time you feel this slipping you should abandon whatever training procedure you are doing or about to do and go back to square one, playing with your dog and working as a team. It works rather in the same way as giving a child encouragement or reward in the middle of a difficult project, it helps give him the will and the drive to carry on.

Sometimes your dog may be a little puzzled at the outset of a new exercise, but continue to break it up into small step by step segments and keep him keen by using your 'want' aids, then he will trust you. Each time he learns to trust you a little more, it makes teaching the next exercise so much more easy. He then knows that he has nothing to fear and that pleasure is always connected with you, thus he will become more receptive each time, and learn to learn.

Heel work comes very naturally to some dogs and handlers, to others it seems like an uphill struggle. Each dog is different, each handler different, so you must learn to be adaptable. I have had some dogs of my own that have, without any formal teaching, automatically taken up the watchful heel position, whilst others have taken a long time to mature and then teach. So even knowing how to do the right things does not always mean that you can do it straight away. It will all come together with trust, maturity, and a willingness to learn on both sides of the partnership.

The next few chapters are all concerning heel work, but the most important thing to achieve before you start is covered in the concepts section, and that is **'The want'**.

Holly keeps a well motivated position, Yvonne's tug toy tooked into her left hand, ready to drop to the dog for reward

The Heel position - what 'Close' means

Before you start - You should have achieved with your dog the 'Want'. It will also be beneficial to teach the sit and the watch.

Keeping the dog in a consistent and correct heel position in the ring can be the difference between winning and loosing in these days of super precise handlers and dogs. So the key word for 'Close' or 'Heel' must mean to the dog, much more than just, 'walk to heel'. *'Close'* must mean, follow my left leg whatever it does, wherever it goes, and stay in a precise and consistent position.

Step one - To teach the word and position *'Close'* we need of course first to be clear of what we are trying to achieve. Secondly the dog must be in a receptive state, so you must work with him to get him in play mode and achieve *'the want'.* Then you can guide him into the heel/close position and gently guide, encourage and motivate him to put his head up to watch you. He will of course be on his lead so you will have complete control. As soon as you have him in the perfect position give your key word *'Close'*, and praise while he is correct and then release.

Heather uses her toy to motivate her puppy Tiffy into the heel position.

73

What 'Close' Means

Initially *'Close'* will mean come into the heel position, and watch me. You should also at this time use your key word *'Watch'* to gain eye contact, gently guiding his head up with your hands or using your toy to get a positive result. Remember to keep this light and fun. To recap the procedure is; play to get the *'Want'*, keep the momentum going, hold your lead in your right hand and slide your left hand down towards the collar to guide the dog into the correct heel position. When the dog is in the correct position give the key word *'Close'*. Guide the head up, better still use your toy as an incentive for the dog to look up. Talk to him to keep his attention on you and use the key word *'watch'*. Take just a couple of steps praising the dog when he is in the correct position, and then give the release word, *'That'll do'*, and play. Repeat this several times to get the dog enjoying the action and gaining momentum. Each time you do the exercise the dog should become more confident, and eager to launch himself into position. The more laid back, quiet, or sensitive the dog the longer you stick to step one, teaching the dog that it is OK to have fun and work with you.

It is up to you to guide the dog into the correct heel position, his shoulders should remain level with your leg. Do not be tempted to allow him too far forward, especially if he is a keen dog. He should not be wrapped around you, or be laying heavily on to you, although it is normal to feel some body contact, particularly whilst the dog is at the early learning stage. You will avoid problems associated with 'Laying on', 'Crabbing', 'Surging', Dipping', and so on, if you follow the techniques in this book and refrain from checking the dog across your body with a lead, or making him unsure of himself by expecting him to cope with things that you have not taught correctly.

Step two - Once the dog is happily coming in to the correct heel position, you can add the sit position at the end or beginning. Therefore step two and three can be done in any order. With the more exuberant dog I find it easier to put in a sit at the beginning, with a dog that becomes more OTT the more you train him, starting at this step gains the initial control. So we are simply following the instructions above but adding a static sit. Start off with the dog in the sit position, go to the end of your lead, and then call him into the close position, take a few steps forward, reward when the dog is in the correct heel position, release and play. Careful positioning of your toy will help to keep the dog in the correct position and to keep his eye on you, so try to keep the toy above his head.

Step three - Now you can introduce a sit position at the end of the exercise. You need not do this every time, but it will start to teach the dog that close means you follow the left leg, if it stops you do to. Follow the instructions as step one, and then instead of just breaking and playing after you have taken a couple of steps, reach back with your right hand and place the dog in the correct heel work sit. His shoulders must be level with your leg. He should be positioned square behind and in front. He should be watching and happy. It takes a little practice for you to get it right, but once you have got it, you should be able to place the dog accurately every time. Then he is learning correctly, and not by correction.

All of this should flow with no obvious breaks. There is no need to give the sit command, as we are teaching a whole procedure on one key word, *'Close'*. The dog is quite capable of achieving this position without even the *'watch'* command, as you can encourage the head up and he will come to associate *'Close'* to mean *'Head up and watch',* as well as the rest. The *'Watch'* key word will be useful later on when you need to gain the dog's attention in differing circumstances. It is a tool for you, an extra key word which the dog understands, and can be used when your handling or the circumstances necessitate. The sit command is not needed because we are teaching the dog to stop and sit immediately the left leg stops, and to come

into a perfectly positioned sit. If you have been training the *'Sit'* position separately you should be getting an instant sit on that key word. Therefore if you give the key word *'Sit'* in the heel position you may indeed get a quick sit but it could also be a crooked sit because the dog should sit were ever he is. So it is better to keep the procedure and the key words as uncomplicated as possible.

Never prolong the teaching session just because it appears to be going well, this will only be inviting error. Be contented with one or two perfect steps so start with, and only increase when you are sure that your dog is understanding, and also enjoying the close position. **Read Your Dog!**

Step four - Once your dog is ultra confident in the close position, you can practise some of the following

Keep good control by holding the lead right down by the collar, keep your attitude and actions pleasant and positive.

tightening up exercises in conjunction with your daily routines. Always start off with play to achieve the *'want'*.

Using the *'Close'* key word, move forward and bring the dog into the close heel position. Use your hands, lead and voice to guide his head and body into the correct position leaving nothing to chance. Next step sideways away from the dog whilst still moving forward. Run your left hand down the lead to the dog's collar to guide him into the close position. Just do it once to begin with but as the dog progresses you can add to the exercise by taking another step forward, and another step sideways, guiding him each time. When the dog becomes confident you can link several paces at a time. Give no aggression or harsh handling just a playful attitude and clear concise movements and words.

Another exercise is to take a few paces with the dog in position, take a quick yet playful turn in the opposite direction, to the left or to the right, again guiding him into the correct position, telling him *'Close'*. The attitude must be that by your side is the best place in the world to be. Never be domineering or forceful with your voice or handling.

You will find many other exercises throughout the book that will reinforce this close position. All of the heel work exercises will be dependent on it and in turn help to teach it. Exercises for the A Recall, the Finish, and various others all have components within them which will help.

Short spurts, broken with play, never over doing it and never tiring or boring your dog. Try left and right handed circles, large ones and then getting smaller, weaving or figure of eight imaginary or placed markers to help you. If the dog is going wrong, stop and go back to the early steps or change direction and bring him in to the correct position. The important thing is not to make it boring and keep that toy or *'want'* aid ready all of the time giving the dog lots of motivation and fun. The section on circuit training will also help you to keep your dog in a happy and stimulated frame of mind.

Remember Read Your Dog!

Gaining these basic skills, gaining the dog's confidence, and enjoying your time with your dog will set you well on the way to being a **Happy Winner.**

Footwork

Foot work is a very important factor of good handling. It is a good idea to perfect this without the dog, rather than drag him around whilst your try to perfect your rhythm and foot placing. The foot patterns that I use are just suggestions, some handlers may choose to use other patterns because of differing physical abilities and or training techniques. The objective is to make sure that the dog understands where you are going from your body posture and foot positioning, so the main criteria is to be the same every time.

The techniques used for teaching the exercises in this book match up to these footwork patterns. If you use others, you must make sure that you are using the correct training techniques with the basis for that being that you will be over exaggerating in training the body posture and footwork that will be used in the ring.

You must concentrate on keeping your body upright, and your head should be facing in the direction that you are going. *(See Deportment).*

Starting and stopping

Often neglected in footwork is the beginning and end of heel work. Your start should be smooth and gliding. Avoid tipping your body forwards. This is often the fault at the start of fast pace. Practice taking your first steps, setting off with your left leg, as this is the first signal to the dog that you are going somewhere. Stopping should be equally smooth. Bring one foot up to the other, normally handlers like to stop on their left foot, and bring the right up to it, but you might like to see which is best for you and your dog on this. Once you have perfected the smooth gliding halt, it probably won't matter which foot you stop on.

The left turn   ### The left about turn

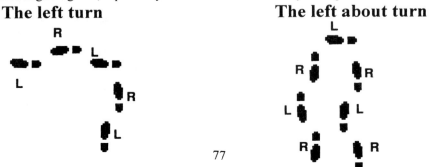

The right turn

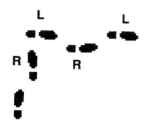

The right about turn

The footwork for circles, weaves and figure of eight, is as normal except that you should be curving your feet in the direction of the pattern.

Footwork can be practised any where, I used to practice at work, when I went out between departments, I have even been known to practice in the supermarket behind a trolley. Turning up and down the isles, placing your feet can be great fun and no one realises what you are doing, and who cares if they do! The more you do it the more natural it becomes. When you have perfected it on your own, get someone to call for you or take a tape recording of a ring steward's voice to follow. It is somewhat harder to start with, when someone else tells you when to turn, but this too will soon become second nature.

Heather Woodford working Crufts OB CH Kirkelly of Stillash showing perfect curving feet.

78

Deportment

When teaching static turns, the heel position, etc., it is very important that you maintain as upright a body stance as physically possible. Accepted, you will need to bend to the dog, especially the smaller dog, but you must constantly tell yourself to keep upright, bottom tucked in and shoulders square pointing the way that you are going. If you don't do this in training, when you come to work your dog in the ring, it will feel so different to the dog that he will think you are in a totally different mood or that the circumstances are different. He will not understand how you want him to work, then all of that training, no matter how good, is wasted. You must aim to have the same body stance and attitude in training as you have in the ring.

It is easy to identify someone who is not the same in themselves, nerves and tension can change the handlers deportment. You need to get a good friend to watch and yell at you if you are not upright, if you are leaning into your dog, or have the famous collie shoulder. When you are trying to perform a good piece of flowing heel work you need to be able to identify if your training posture is different to your handling posture. If you have worked on deportment in training then, even if you are nervous in the ring, to some extent you will feel the same to the dog because your body stance will be right. The dog will then have something concrete to latch on to.

Some handlers are very verbal and lively in training, but then are unable to be the same

Upright handling gets the best results as Janet Matthews demonstrates with Rookie

Deportment

person when someone is watching. Adjust your training to suit your personality. If you know that you find it hard to be extrovert in public then learn to handle in a quieter manner in training. The dog's hearing is far greater than ours, you don't need to screech and shout, try whispering to your dog, see how he responds. Use your toy, your common bond to reward the dog, once the dog is hooked on a toy your input can be minimal giving you time to concentrate on yourself. Find a happy medium where you can cope in public, and train in the same way. The dog will soon learn to respond to the quieter you in training and so it will be easier for him to read you when you are at a show.

The same attitude and procedure applies in the set exercises, retrieve, DC, SA, etc., as your training progresses work on maintaining the upright body posture that you will use in the ring. Use the same sort of actions, words and signals each time, don't change your routine of setting the exercise up when your get within the ring ropes. In training don't let the dog fly off in-between exercises, you won't be able to do that in the ring, keep the fun next to you.

Practise on your own just as you would with footwork, to get a natural, even, balanced gait until you feel comfortable with it. Use a *pace setter* to create a regular pace. The more you do it, the more natural it will become. Watch other handlers, see how the good ones bend and straighten as a natural progression, and their body is upright most of the time. Always become upright when the dog is in a working position even when training. The best place to watch is in the car park when handlers are warming up. But beware don't take on board everything you might see in the car park, some handler's attitudes to the dog leave a lot to be desired!

So to recap; Keep upright, develop a natural, even, gait, be the same in training as you intend to be in the ring. Shoulders back, body facing the direction in which you are going, tuck your bottom in, don't slouch into the corners, turn keeping your body square - Aim to flow!

Eliminating Aids

One of the most common excuses given to me by handlers for not using motivational aids such as toys and/or titbits in training is that you can not take them into the ring. My answer to that is that you can't use any of the other aids for training in the ring either. You can't use lead control in any class, voice and signal control are limited to the start of each exercise in the higher classes. Nevertheless handlers still quite rightly use leads, hands, voice and other things for teaching their dogs. The aids will not be effective unless coupled with sufficient motivation.

Everyone has to learn how to eliminate aids what ever method of teaching they might use. Aids should be gradually reduced and substituted in such a way that the dog does not miss them and expect that they might appear any moment. It is better that these aids are friendly if we wish to remain friends with the dog. In the case of body and verbal signals, it is best to train with a minimal amount, thus there are less to eliminate! The key words and aids that you use should be simple and effective.

Each training procedure covered in the *techniques* section will be made up of many aids to assist you and the dog to get it right. These aids should never be dropped all at once. The biggest mistakes come when novice handlers win out of the class and decide to work test 'A'. They seem to go immediately dumb, poker stiff, unable to aid their dog and bad tempered! The temper is lost through frustration, the sudden inability to do well is most embarrassing and takes some living down. From the dog's point of view the world has become very puzzling. Once he had noise and help galore, all of a sudden his time within the ring ropes has become akin to entering a different world. The dog does not have to go through this, nor does the handler, if training and motivation are approached in a straight forward and honest manner.

Body Posture and Footwork

When teaching a dog we should aim where possible, to make sure that the first thing the dog sees is the natural body posture which will be allowable in the ring.

81

Eliminating Aids

This helps the dog to read you, and also helps him to adjust himself ready for the next action. To give you an example; when training the left turn in heel work, and progressing to putting things together on the move, the first thing the dog should see and feel is your body posture altering, followed by your leading foot, (normally your left foot), going into the turn. This is then followed up by your hand going down the lead towards the collar, and a step back on your right foot which over exaggerates the body posture in the ring. (*See left turns section for more details of this turn*). This principle is followed in all exercises, and the aids gradually dropped, but each basic training procedure will always be started with the only thing that will be left for the dog to see in the ring, when the aids are dropped.

Verbal Commands

The section on *Voice - Tones and Usage,* will help you greatly in understanding how to use words, which is an important factor in learning how to eliminate those extra words that mean the loss of points in the ring. A dog's concentration span must be gradually worked upon. Most people who read this section of the book will be at least aiming beyond beginners. You cannot simply become quiet and go marching off into the distance expecting the dog, who is used to a fairly constant banter from you, to stay accurately by your side in the heel position. Your first task is to make sure that the dog understands the key words and has learnt to perform the exercises on the utterance of just the one word, with a little extra help and encouragement where necessary.

Once we are sure that the dog understands we can then use the reward training, be it toy or food to gradually extend the length of time that the dog works without the handler having to say anything. This must be done just as all of your training, in stages. The key words should not really be repeated once the dog is performing correctly, the key words are tools to tell the dog what to do next. To repeat them really serves very little purpose. They will need encouragement only, if your training is thorough. If at any time the dog looks confused or worried you should go back to your game to regain his confidence, put in some basic training help, and then the next time, don't try to keep going for so long.

Each individual exercise, giving you suggestions of what words to use, is dealt with in it's own section, taking you from basics to more advanced. The main criteria for eliminating commands is to make sure that your dog is taught to perform the task on one simple key word, he will be aided with your consistent body posture, pleasant confident attitude and tone of voice. Eliminating word usage need not be a major stumbling block for you and your dog.

Toys and Titbits

The use of motivational aids such as toys and titbits is a crucial element in all of the concepts and training methods in this book, and indeed of most modern training techniques. The sections on *Timing* and *Rewards* will have given you the information that you need on how to use them. To get rid of them is a gradual process. As far as the dog is concerned they will never go completely, he will merely learn to expect them less often.

It is scientific fact that if you teach an animal to expect to be rewarded, and then withhold that reward, as long as he is aware and has been programmed where the reward might come, he will work faster and harder to get to the next reward. This is the principle behind limiting and spacing out your rewards.

Step one - Let's say for instance that you have been teaching heel work with a toy lure. The dog has reached the point where he is happy trotting along in the heel position, with his eyes fixed firmly on his toy. The first stage to elimination would be to enclose your hand around the toy to hide it from view, the dog obviously knows that it is still there. Take a few paces like this and then reveal it to the dog, and then reward with the toy and release.

Step two - Get the dog back into heel work mode with your toy, when he is well motivated, move it behind your back for a few seconds only and then reveal again, while the dog is still working, and then reward and release.

Step three - Get the dog in heel work mode with your toy and then casually put the toy in your pocket for a few seconds. No more than a few seconds should elapse before you bring the toy back out, still with the dog working, and then reward and release.

Step four - Repeat the above three stages,

Yvonne Hollyoak works Sealight Jimmy using a toy half covered by her hand

increasing gradually the time that the toy is out of sight. Do not progress too quickly as we do not want to bore the dog, or make him lose interest. Be ready at any time to bring the toy back if necessary. Keep it exciting and do not be tempted to change your attitude. Everything should remain the same, you voice your body stance, etc. The only thing that differs is that the toy is not always in sight, but it soon reappears.

If the dog is distracted at any time, don't yell, shout, check or drag him about, simply get out your toy and turn in the opposite direction to the distraction, taking the dog enthusiastically with you. Your attitude should be one of sheer amazement that the dog could possibly find anything more riveting than you. Turn on the charm!

Step five - Soon the dog will be able to work for longer stretches with a minimum of input from your toy. When you are sure he is becoming confident try putting the toy on a table, without the dog seeing to start with. Do a little heel work and then work in the direction of the table, collecting the toy, reward him. If he loses concentration or is distracted at this point then you should consider that you have not spent long enough on the above stages.

Don't ever get to the stage where you eliminate the reward completely, the dog should always assume that there is one just around the corner.

This gradual weaning technique can be applied to all of the exercises, and the toy then becomes the reward for correct behaviour instead of merely a lure.

Heel work - sits

If you have taught the *'Close'* key word correctly you will not need to worry unduly about sits in heel work, except to make sure that you are always in a position to ensure their accuracy. In teaching the word *'Close'* we have taught the dog that whatever the left leg does, he follows. If the leg turns he goes neatly with it and if the leg stops then he sits squarely by its side. We have, as a separate exercise, taught him that sit means sit immediately. If given that command in heel work, then that is what he should do, i.e. sit immediately. Now, if your timing is **not** impeccable or the dog steps onto an uneven piece of ground and his body swaggers slightly, this could mean a crooked sit. But, by giving him his *'Close'* key word as you come to a halt, he will know to took himself neatly in by your side in the correct heel position. Remember to keep your body upright and to bring your feet together smoothly to give him the best chance of understanding what you want.

Try to avoid doing long stretches of heel work and lots of sits. When training for sits, do a few paces and then guide the dog in to the correct heel position. Place him each time with your hands, or use your titbit/reward to guide his head up and keep his body straight. With larger dogs you can use a wall to make sure that they do not topple over to one side. Use your knowledge to ensure

Take complete control with your lead and hands - position the dog correctly so that he learns what is wanted.

that the dog is always correctly positioned in training, and this will avoid him assuming that anything else is acceptable.

If the dog develops faults along the way look to your basic training of the *'Close'* command. Probably you have become a little less thorough than you should be in your warm up routines, and need to do more regular ground work. It does not hurt, in fact it has very positive results if you refrain from putting the heel work together at every session. So if faults occur i.e. slow, crooked, wrapped, whatever, go back to basic routines only, and then progress slowly eliminating aids one at time and then and keeping up the momentum in training, before putting things together ready for the ring. Remember your master piece can be unveiled in the ring you do not have to keep having sneak previews to see if you've got it right!

Heel Work Turns

Left turn - the basic procedure

Before you start the dog must already understand - how to play - and know what to associate with the key words 'Sit', 'Close', 'Watch' and 'Good boy'.

Step one - As always start with play and achieve *'the Want'*. Once you have the dog keen and receptive place him in the sit position by your side (on lead of course). Tell him to *'Sit'*, *'Doggy SIT'*, leave him taking a pace to your right and a pace or so forward. Stand side on to your dog, hold the end of your lead and your toy or *'want'* aid in your right hand, now simultaneously step back with your right leg, run your left hand down the lead near to the dog's collar, and guide the dog into the heel position. Take a step or two forward with the dog in the heel position and then use your toy to reward as you release and give your key word, *'OK'*, followed with lots of enthusiastic praise. When you have mastered the technique introduce the *'close'* command. During the exercise use your reward words *'good boy'* to give the dog confidence. There is no need at this stage to put in a sit position at the end of the exercise, because what you are trying to achieve is a good, neat, flowing left turn.

Many handlers will be used to moving the left leg back to teach this turn and whilst this does work, I find that moving the right leg is imitating and overemphasising the body stance

Flash has his full attention on Sheila, her left hand is ready to run down the lead to guide him into the left.

that the dog will be working to when you are working in the ring.

Whilst you are teaching the dog the turns it is a good idea to a make sure that you can do them yourself. *(See Footwork)*

Step two - Once the dog is happily coming in to the heel position from approximately a lead's length away, you can shorten the distance that you leave him a step at a time. Eventually you will be just turning side on to him, and ultimately turning left on the spot. Always use all of your aids, your voice, your lead, your hands, and your *'want'* aid. Never go too fast for the dog, only progress as fast as the dog can cope, and at each session start from the beginning, working up to the previous session's level and then moving on a little when you and the dog are ready. Even when you consider that the dog is completely trained always start from the beginning at each training session to remind him what is wanted. This way you will maintain the accuracy ready for the ring.

Step three - There are variations on the theme that will help the dog to understand what is wanted form him. Leave the dog in the sit position, go to the end of your lead, and take a couple of steps to the right, stand side on to the dog, run your hand down the lead to the collar, take a step back with your right leg and guide the dog into the heel position. Once you have perfected the technique put in your key words.

Once the dog is well on the way to performing the turn accurately from a standstill, you can start to teach him to put it together in heel work. This is a most important stage of the left turn that is often forgotten by handlers in their rush to be ready for the ring.

On the Move

Remembering and being well practised in your footwork will make it so much easier for the dog to perform accurate turns, making it the same for him each time will give both of you a much better chance of getting it right. Make sure you have the dog's full attention by getting *'the want'*, and then with the lead and your *'want'* aid in your right hand, give your heel command and take a few paces forward with the dog encouraging him to join you in heel work. When you feel comfortable simultaneously give your close command *'Leo close'*, turn your left foot across the dog and swivel your body to the left, step back with your right foot, run your left hand down the lead and guide the dog back with a circular movement into the heel position, use your voice and *'Want'* aid to keep his head up and concentrating on you and take one or two steps forwards only, break the exercise with your release command and play.

Again no need for any sits either at the start or the finish be aware of what you are teaching all of the time and do not clutter the exercise with other things. It is not necessary to give a different command to teach your dog turns because we are aiming for him to take his signal from body posture and footwork only in the long run, another command is another to be dropped at a later stage, so it is better to keep things as uncluttered as possible. It is important to make sure that your foot work is constant and that you remain as upright as possible, otherwise you may well find that you have to completely re-train both your dog and yourself when you need to drop your commands.

Dropping the aids

At this point many people become unstuck, because they try to drop all of the aids at once particularly if they do rather better than they expected and win out of classes quickly. Remember that at each training session start from the beginning, use all of your aids, and work through. Then one at a time aids can be dropped. By this I don't mean a gradual progression leaving nothing to help the dog, but rather drop one, and then put it back and drop another. For instance, as you take the left turn on the move you would call the dog in to heel, (still on lead of course and with your *'want'* aid, these are always the last guidance aids to go), foot across the dog, hand down the lead guiding the dog back, step back, use the dog's name, but drop the keyword, *'close'* . Your foot turning across in front of the dog and your body posture will always be the same as they are your signals in the ring so they must remain constant. Dropping the key word *'close'* first will probably be the least noticed by the dog. Next time leave in the command but take out the step back, or rather make it less obvious by making it a small step instead of a pace. Next time put back the pace and drop or make less obvious the hand movement down the lead, and so on. Don't forget to keep up the *'want'* using your toy and your voice, and you must break in between every section, sooner if necessary and play. As the dog progresses these play sessions need only be fractions of the time that you spent originally, but only you can decide when your dog is ready, if you over do the play or reward it will become boring you must, **Read Your dog.**

Left about turns

The left about turn is a progression of the left turn and is often unnecessarily feared in the ring, if taught correctly with patience and following the correct procedure all able-bodied dogs and handlers can perform the turn with style, the more agile dogs can even perform a good accurate left about turn at the fast pace, although the rules do not necessitate this. It really is just an extension of the left turn, and once your dog is happy doing lefts it will be taken as great fun when you continue turning. The most important thing to remember if you want accuracy in the ring is to make sure that you do the same each time. This means getting your body posture and footwork spot on. *(See Footwork)*

Once you have your dog happily performing the left turn on the spot it quite a simple matter to carefully place your feet and turn a 180° turn, the dog may be a little unsure at first but simply use your lead, voice and toy to give him confidence and guide him back, most dogs will derive great enjoyment from completing a full 360° turn in this manner, and of course over emphasising the turn in training will mean that 180° in the ring presents no problem at all.

To help promote fluid and agile backward movement such as is necessary for the this turn to be executed correctly, the following exercises can be added to your training routines.

The twizzle. This can be done to start with just on its own as a game, but as the handler becomes more proficient it can be incorporated into heel work and turns. It is simply as it suggests, the dog is taken in a 360° circle in an anti-clockwise direction, guided by the lead and in a fun manner. It can be started by using your toy and allowing the dog to follow it around, keep the circle tight and yet wide enough to make sure the dog follows it. So the toy and the lead in the left hand and guide the dog around, give it a key word *'Twizzle'*, and have some fun with your dog.

The Incentive. On a similar vein use the toy to give the dog incentive to be fast on the turns by throwing it behind you as you turn left across the dog, the dog should follow the ball or toy by turning anti-clockwise away from your leg as in the *'twizzle'*. Remember to drop the lead to allow the dog to get the toy, but immediately call him back to you, do not throw the ball to far as you want to maintain the 'fun as a team' aspect, if you give him too much distance fun could start to be better away from you.

Walking backwards, and encouraging the dog to do the same on lefts will also help to promote the close backward movements as will multiple turns on the spot or at random during heel work

All of the extra exercises can be done once the dog has the basic idea of the left, and remember, variety is the spice of life, keep it fun and keep it lively.

Heel Work Turns
Right turns - the basic procedure

Before you start - the dog must understand how to play - and know what to associate with the key words 'Sit', 'Close', 'Watch', and 'Good boy'.

The right turn is often taken for granted until faults, usually going wide or drifting, loosing position etc. occur. Then handlers try to correct those faults instead of training the turn correctly. A dog who has been taught by correction rather than by guidance into the correct performance stands out a mile when you are judging. Even the good ones weave and drift in and out of position, and are constantly correcting them selves, because this is what they have been inadvertently taught to do. Allowing faults to occur teaches the dog that it is okay. Even when he is corrected he has no way of knowing that the first part was wrong, and he will think that this is the procedure which you want him to follow, moving in and out of position as he has been allowed and then corrected. It is much better to teach correctly in the first place don't you think? It certainly saves some heartache on your part, stress on the dog and ink for the judge!

Step one - Play with your dog and get him in a receptive mood. Place him in the sit, 'Leo Sit', go to the end of your lead facing away from the dog. Take a step back with your left leg, slide your left hand down the lead towards the collar to get good control and then with a forward movement call the dog into the heel position 'Leo Close'. Place your left foot across your right as shown in the footwork diagrams, *(See Footwork),* and guide the dog hand still low by the collar and using lead, voice, toy etc. Take a couple of paces forward and break the exercise. Remember there is no need for sits at the finish as we want the timing to be right to reward for the turn.

Step two - The distance leaving the dog can be lessened gradually until eventually he will confidently go with you as you place your feet for the right turn on the spot.

Step three - Right about turn (180° turn to your right). As with left about turns, the right about turn is just an extension of the 45° turn. Commence as at the basic start of the right turn and simply place your feet, *(see footwork section diagrams),* all the way around guiding the dog with lead, voice and play. Remember take only a step or two after the turn and break the exercise. Reward the dog during the turn with your voice, and or encourage him with his toy or a titbit so that he knows he is correct. Do not sit him to finish, we are teaching turns not sits!

Step four - Further exercises can be incorporated once the dog knows what he is doing to help speed up and emphasise the turn: -

1) Play with the dog and then call him into the heel position take one or two steps and then turn to the right, (45 or 180 degrees). Take one or two steps forwards encouraging the dog and then praise and play. Remember to place your feet correctly and keep your body posture upright, and help the dog every step of the way rewarding him during the exercise with your voice to give him confidence.

2) Take a few steps forwards with your dog about turn and then back off and call your dog as if you were teaching him a basic recall, bring out the ball or toy to heighten the excitement. Swivel the dog back into heel work for a few steps and then repeat the procedure.

Mary Griffiths prepares to call Boswell into the right

3) With more advanced dogs go into the about turn but then step side ways or backwards and quickly guide the dog into the correct position encourage him to be more attentive to the close heel position.

4) A few steps of heel work and then double about turn, as he completes the double turn toss your toy in the direction that he has been following, i.e. round to the right, to give him a motivation boost.

As always keep it simple, fun and ever changing. Do not bore your dog. Even high fun activities will loose their appeal if you repeat them too often.

Read Your Dog

Paces: Slow, Fast, Normal

Before you start - your dog should be happily working at normal pace, as covered in previous chapters.

Many unnecessary marks are lost during slow and fast paces in heel work. Major faults comprise of; the handler launching their bodies into the start of fast, stumbling into the start of slow, being uneven in their movements, not taking turns smoothly, being ring shy, and forgetting all that they ever learnt about footwork and deportment, not keeping a constant speed, etc., etc.

You will notice that I don't blame the dog in any of this, after all *he* is only following *your* lead. Dogs do tend to develop particular idiosyncrasies like getting over excited, barking, or lagging etc., but these faults are caused by the handlers not getting themselves together in the ring and/or in training. The more that the problems and inaccuracies are ignored or left to 'Go away on their own', the worse or more exaggerated they can become.

To teach your dog to do varying paces accurately is very much an extension of normal, walking pace heel work.

Pace Setters

It is important to develop a rhythmic pace that the dog can come to rely on. There are various ways of getting your pace right. There is now available an electronic pace setter, which can be set to the perfect pace for you and your dog. Once you have decided on the best setting for you and the dog as a team, you simply set the instrument and practice along with the rhythmic beat both with your dog and without. Training yourself this way will help the consistency and quality of your pace.

Step one - To perfect your paces, and to ensure that the dog goes into them evenly, proceed as follows. Without your dog to start with, learn to change paces so that there is obvious change. This must be observable distinctly to those that are watching, without being unduly slow or fast.

Paces

Don't attempt for instance, to do the sort of fast pace that you could not keep up for any length of time, in any case you may have to train and build up your own stamina to enable you to maintain an acceptable speed. It is better to get a good rhythm, a jog for example, than trying to run at full pelt if you are not built for it. Like wise with slow pace do not be too slow, practice to become consistent. You may decide to change the speeds slightly when you get together with your dog, but this self-training will give you a basis to work on.

Step two - Assuming that you have your dog working happily and confidently at the normal pace, and you have completed step one, we can now start to train the dog to enjoy the variations of pace. Place the dog in the sit position or simply call him into the heel position using his name and your key word, *'Close'*. He will of course be on lead, because we are training, you can use all of your help aids, and of course you know by now that your *'Want'* aid should always be in your hand or in your pocket at the ready. Once the dog is happily and accurately trotting at your side in the heel position, gradually and smoothly glide into the slow pace. Just do a few steps reassuring the dog all of the time, and then just as smoothly glide back into normal pace. Break the exercise with your release command and then play. Repeat this several times playing and encouraging where necessary.

Step three - The procedure as in step two should be followed to introduce fast pace. Remember of course to keep your body upright and make sure your footwork is spot on. The tendency is for handlers, particularly at fast pace, to let their legs fly all over the place. So remember, keep your knees together on those turns, and keep it smooth. It helps of course particularly at fast pace if you are reasonably fit, but you can train yourself to glide even if you are a little on the rotund side. Always be ready to break and play at any time that the dog needs it .

Step four - Practice the turns placing your feet just as you would in normal pace. Remember, take smaller steps out of the turn to help the dog hold the correct position. Keep it rhythmic and positive and the dog will hold position more easily.

Some time ago I judged a lady who came into my 'C' ring, she was very large to say the least and I expected to see her give a show of very erratic fast pace, but I was amazed when she turned in one of the best heel work rounds of the day, putting slimmer more athletic types to shame, she

94

had obviously taught herself to *glide!*

Slow and fast pace from a stand still

In test B the change of pace is always from the standstill, in some ways this is harder than on the changes on the move which don't occur until test C. To perfect the differing paces from a stand still is however a simple procedure, if you approach it in a simple manner. Get your dog in the right frame of mind with a little well motivated heel work. Halt and place him in the correct heel sit position. Before you set off into the slow or fast pace give the dog's name in a differing tone to usual so that he is aware that something is to be different. The slow can be a calm slow tone, the fast a quicker more exciting one. Follow it up with the key word, *'Close'* in the same tone, and then smoothly glide into your chosen pace. Be careful not to lunge forward with your body in fast pace, because the dog is likely to surge forward with your posture; and be very positive as you move off in slow, to avoid hesitation and dipping.

Circles, Weaves & Figure of Eight

Before you start - The dog needs to have the want, and understand what 'Close' means.

Teaching the dog in circles is the way we often start in the early stages of training, to get a flow of heel work. When we comes to use these techniques for working in the ring it seems much harder. The reason is that once the dog starts to be able to hold a good position in the straight heel work, the handler gets carried away teaching twists and turns, and the circles tend to be forgotten until suddenly they are needed when the handler is approaching the level of test 'B' or 'C'.

The techniques for circles and curving heel work are just the same as straight, but the handler will have to learn how to point his feet and body into the curve. *(See Footwork and Deportment).*

Start training with large circles, and accustom yourself to how if feels to not be going in a straight line. Try not to lean over the dog, but to keep an upright torso. As you progress you can go in slightly tighter circles, if you feel the dog coming to far across you or hanging back straighten up, revert to the opposite curve, or go into play mode to get the dog's confidence. Normally the handler has more trouble coping

Heather Woodford with Kelly using a hool-a-hoop to train around at summer camp

96

Circles, Weaves and Figure of Eight

with curving heel work than the dog. Any turn should be done with exactly the same footwork as the straight turns.

You will probably find it easier, at least to start with, to teach the curves at slow pace. The dog should be very attentive and more easily controlled at slow, with less tendencies to surge out of position whilst you are teaching and adjusting yourself. Once you get to grips with it, start to smarten your pace, until you are able to keep a consistent pace all the way around. It is important that you teach yourself to keep as consistent a pace as possible and then pass this over to the dog.

You must also accustom yourself to going into the curves from the straight, and from a standstill. Sometimes judges will include in their tests, curves at the various paces, and also execute about turns to bring you back into the opposite curve. All of this is really quite easy for the dog that has been taught correctly to start with, all of the techniques used in this book will teach the dog to follow the left leg. It is the handler who will have to be strict with himself and learn to get his deportment and footwork correct, and there is no easy option other than *training yourself.*

When you start to get the hang of this, introduce actual markers to accustom the dog to ignore the obstacle, and to accustom yourself to being more specific and structured with regards to which direction you go, and how you follow a set pattern. Children's hool-a-hoops are ideal training aids, but also bollards, poles etc., can be used to give you the right feel. *Circuit training* will help you with this, because you can set up your training area to either use or not use the obstacles.

Positions on the move (ASSD)
(Advanced stand, sit and down)

Before you start - The dog must understand key words for sit, down, stand, heel, watch, and have achieved the want. He must be happy and confident in the heel position with no signs of apprehension or confusion. You must understand what you are trying to achieve.

Think carefully about what you are trying to achieve. You will need to teach the dog to give a positive immediate reaction to your key word. In the ring the dog must stop in his tracks and assume the position given. Then he must wait without moving or fidgeting until invited to re-join you in the correct heel position. The first part you must achieve is for the dog to stop and assume the position given; for this the dog needs to understand fully what is meant by the key words, stand, sit and down, or signals that mean the same. *(See each individual position, for teaching methods.)* Your dog must be very happy and confident when working in the heel position before you start introducing this exercise, other wise he may become unsure and hesitant in his heel work. Having said that, you don't have to wait until you qualify for the standard. If you have an ultra keen dog, teaching ASSD can help to keep him under control, giving him something more to keep his mind occupied, and preventing heel work from getting boring.

Step one - Take things as usual, one step at a time. Decide on what position you would like to start with, the sit or the down are probably easiest, but if your basic training is good, then any position will do. Let us say that you will start with the Sit position. Remember your general training procedure, get the dog *'wanting'* before you start, use your *'want'* aid, and of course keep him on lead. When you are ready call him into the heel position to join you as you walk forward, *'Leo Close, Good boy'.* Shorten your lead up in your right hand, and when you are confident that you are going to get a good result, simply but swiftly raise your right hand with your lead upwards keeping the lead short. Place your left hand on the dog's rump, just as you would in basic training. The secret is that you should not to come to a formal stop before you place him. The object is to imitate as much as possible the position and body posture taken in the ring, leaving the dog behind as you walk forwards. Take a couple of paces away from the dog. Hold the lead high above the dog's head to make sure that he doesn't break the position. Reassure him, return to his side and break the exercise with your release command, and play. Repeat this a few times until you are sure of what you are doing and can get it right most times and then introduce your key word *'Sit'*.

Step two - The other two positions are taught in exactly the same way, using your basic teaching and aids to ensure that the dog assumes the correct position. You can use your lead to stop the dog in his tracks for the stand position, your hand signal may help coming across the dog's face to make a very positive action. For the down simply come straight down on the dog's shoulders with your left hand to manipulate him into position or in front of his nose if you have used the titbit/incentive down method of teaching. Make sure that your physical signals and your verbal key words are used in exactly the same manner as they will be used in the ring. If your tone or action changes the dog will not understand.

Step three - As the dog begins to gain confidence you will be able to extend the time that you leave him in the position. First work on circling around the dog, again using your lead and your voice to make sure he remains static in the correct position. If he attempts to break or shuffle around to see you go back a few steps and be happy to just stand in front of him until he gains more confidence. Always complete the training session with a game, and of course break in between each segment and produce your *'want'* aid. Plenty of time should be spent on this stage of the training to make sure that the dog is really attuned to what you want. Gradually you will be able to drop the aids, remembering that you should only drop one bit of help at a time, and then replace it before dropping another.

Preparing for the ring

Make sure that your key words are precise and clear, and of course the same every time. Make sure your body posture is upright, and that you can give your commands without leaning over the dog. The pick up part is easy if your basic training has been thorough. To start with, pause as you come into the heel position, and then give the dog your *'Close'* key word and encourage him forward for a few steps.

To avoid anticipation in the ring learn to be varied in training, sometimes picking up by giving the *'close'* command, but more often walking past, taking an acute turn in front of the dog or simply going to his side and releasing him. Don't always release and go forward sometimes release and go backwards or sideways. You will need to practice your own timing to get a perfect pickup. Remember to always make sure that the dog is happy and confident, and at the least sign of apprehension break and play, then start again at an easier level.

Heel Work - Trouble Shooting

Forward Working

Once upon a time forward working was rarely a problem, as a judge most faults witnessed were those related to lagging behind.   Now-a-days there is much more emphasis on reward based training, but the control element of the training tends to get lost amongst the high exuberance sometimes.   Forward working is normally created by the fun approach to dog training being used with out suitable control being implemented.   The dog will be continually allowed to lunge forward for his reward which the handler has a tendency to give at the end of the exercise.   He is unable to perceive the correct heel position because he is rewarded when he is in the wrong position each time.   It is normal animal behaviour to try to get to the reward. When you withdraw a reward, the dog will try to get as fast as possible to the point at which the reward comes. The withdrawal of the reward will emphasise this, so although we need to learn to eliminate rewards, we must also learn *when* to reward. *(See Timing and Reward Training).*

Piper is a very exuberant dog, but also quite sensitive. When he is held away he is very keen to get into the correct position.

Let's take the example of the very keen, over excitable dog. He will display all of the classic symptoms.   Lively, raring to go, but often will be really quite sensitive.   The handler will have found that reprimanding the dog has no suitable effect, so it is obvious that there is need for a more constructive approach.

100

Heel Work - Trouble Shooting

Technique one

Step one - The exercise must be broken down again into segments. Set the dog up in the heel position and reward him by stroking his head or if you are using a toy for his motivator drop it into his mouth whilst he is in the correct position. Often with over keen dogs it is useful to use your voice a lot instead of continually rewarding with the toy, so that he learns to feel rewarded in a more controlled manner. But, you should not eliminate his toy completely, he must learn to give and take. *(See Teaching the Keen Dog)*

Step two - Set the dog up again and this time take one step with him, if he holds position reward him, whilst he is correct. This is the hard part to get under control, because the dog will have grown accustomed to surging forward to gain his reward. You may find, to start with at least, that it is easier to place the dog into the sit after one perfect step, and then reward him. Try not to do this for too long, or otherwise the dog will start to think that reward comes only when he is sitting! If you miss and the dog surges, slide your left hand down his lead to his collar and hold him out away from you for a few seconds. Give him a disappointed look, say *'What are you doing?'* in a voice that tells him that you are not happy, but yet is **not** loud and aggressive, he will want to come back to you so now is your chance to make it happen under control, bring the dog back into the correct position and reward him in position, *'Good boy'.*

Step three - You must now follow this technique, every time the dog surges forward, hold him away for a few seconds, bring back and reward the correct position. Keep going back to the beginning so that the dog gains nothing from his surge, but is rewarded in the correct position.

Technique two

Step one - Bring your dog into the heel position. Take a step forward, the fraction of a second that the dog starts to go forward from the correct heel position, start walking backwards bringing the dog back towards you on your left, the keen dog will quickly try to back to you, reel him and make him go past you on your left, and as soon as he is heading past, start walking forwards again bringing him into position. There is no need to say a word, whilst he is wrong, but as soon as he reaches the correct heel position, give him his key word *'Close',* and tell him *'Good boy'.* If you are using a toy reward him when he is correct.

Step two - Set it up again. The dog will come into the correct position, but will soon start to race forward again, the second that he is forward, simply stop walk back and bring him into the correct position as above. The important part to remember is to act the fraction of a second that the dog is in the incorrect position. If you allow some forward work the dog will not know when to do it and when not, and will become confused. You must make up your mind that the dog will not forward work ever again, if you want him to maintain a good position in the ring.

This technique can also be used on dogs that pull, even pet handlers can master it. The dog will learn with a minimum of input from the handler, that he can't go forward unless he does it in the position that the handler allows, it is up to the handler to decide on the position that is acceptable, and only go forward when the dog is there. It may seem that you are not getting very far, especially if you are stopping a dog pulling on walk, but it will be worth it and soon the dog will realise how to walk to heel.

Inconsistent heel position

This is one of the top faults in the obedience ring, dogs that have a fluctuating heel position. The only way to correct this is to make sure that you are teaching the dog correctly, and not by **correction,** show the dog exactly what is wanted, and teach every exercise step by step, rewarding each tiny piece and progressing to the stage where the dog is not quite sure what order things will come, but knows how to react to your signals and keywords. If the dog gives the incorrect reaction to your signal or word, simply go back to step one of the training exercise and teach the dog exactly what you do mean

You must learn to be very controlled in you deportment and handling, so that the dog does not misconstrue your body or foot movement, but more importantly the dog must be given a controlled approach to all of the heel work teaching.

By following all of the techniques the dog will learn the correct position, you must not teach with aggression because this will make the dog very 'dippy', and inclined to drop out of position in case your hand is on the way down.

Many inconstancies in position are caused by handlers not following the handling techniques which are compatible with their footwork and deportment in the ring. In training your techniques should start by presenting yourself in an over exaggeration of the finished product. So for instance if you are doing a turn in training your body should show the same but exaggerated shape that the dog will see in the ring. Then as the training procedure progresses, you will tighten up the posture to leave only what the dog will see. Inconsistency comes with uncertainty, over excitement, and incorrect training or training by correction.

Lagging

Dogs lag for various reasons, one of the major causes is that they are not motivated sufficiently to stay with the handler. Apprehensive and sensitive dogs are more likely to lag as are larger more cumbersome dogs. These dogs cannot be taught by aggression, because this will make their motivation level even more difficult to uplift. The lagging dog needs a positive, controlled and highly motivated trainer. He needs to be shown exactly where he is meant to be, and what he is meant to do in a manner that he can understand and in the nicest possible way. His motivator must be chosen to suit his character.

Constant nagging on the lead will make the dog even more inclined to hold back, often it is as well to dispense with the lead for a while and teach the dog that the heel position is a fun place to be. You can if you are able to retrain yourself, teach the dog that the lead has good associations and even teach him to play with it as explained at the beginning of 'the Want.'

Bad body posture will also cause lagging . If the handler looks down at the dog, with his head turned to the side, the rest of the body has a tendency to follow. This gives a false impression of the heel position and the dog ends up a few paces behind. The usual reaction from the handler is then to chastise or nag with the lead because he is annoyed at the dog, this is done by turning even further into the dog. Once this happens and the dog loses all continuity and faith and it becomes more natural for him to get even further back than to come forward. Think about how you would teach a dog to lag and this is probably a variation on what you are doing to try to correct it!

To correct lagging you need to teach and motivate from the beginning. Do **not** try to make it right by correction because the dog will not understand, and will become even less likely to want to stay with you. Change your key words if you have abused them, and teach the dog good associations.

Wide turns

Two things to look at here; a) is your footwork and deportment correct, and b) have you taught the turns correctly.

a) Footwork and deportment must be compatible with your training methods. Check this first in the techniques chapter applicable. The dog must understand what is meant when your body and feet take up certain positions. Even your head and facial expressions will make a difference. Make sure that your head follows the turn and does not get left behind because you have one eye on the dog. Make sure you are accustomed to turning when told to avoid errors. Get others to analyse what you do or watch on video if possible.

b) Often handlers start to teach turns but do not follow the procedure through and/or do not continue to train rather than handle in training sessions. Progressing to the 'on the move aids' is often the stage at which training gets left behind in favour of handling, this must not happen if you want to keep your turns tight and accurate.

Crooked sits

Three areas to look at here; a) Crooked sits can be avoided by never allowing them to creep in training. b) Bad body posture and foot work can once again be the culprit that sends potentially good sits crooked. c)Use of incorrect verbal commands in the ring will also confuse the dog.

a) In training always place the dog into the correct sit position at your side. The sits should be taught to start with as a separate exercise and only incorporated into heel work in linking sessions. Remember to pay attention to what you are trying to teach, and make sure that you brain is in gear.

b) Do not lean over or come stomping to a halt as this will again affect the dog, and make him apprehensive or confused. Make sure that you glide to a halt and keep your body upright, bend back to place the dog, or use a wall to avoid the crooked position if necessary.

c)Do not introduce the key word 'sit' in heel work if you have followed the techniques in this book, because you will have taught the dog to sit instantly on that word. So when he hears it in heel work, if your training is good, he will sit, whatever position he finds his body in. If he needs an extra keyword in the ring then the word should be 'Close'.

Slow sits

Both keen and not so keen dog suffer from slow sits. Keen because they are rearing to go and the slower dog for obvious reasons. Both can be dealt with in a similar manner. The dog must have motivation to get into the sit position, find what it is that your dog likes and use it as a reward for quick and stable sits. With the keen dog this is usually a fairly easy task as he is easily motivated, but the slower dog take more patience. Do not wait to do some heel work to try this; teach separately. When the dog is sitting reward him. Do your training little and often so that the dog starts to enjoy going into the sit, introduce a sequence of sit, stand, down and reward the sit more often than the rest. This shouldn't be DC style, just a bit of fun as you might teach pet dogs with a titbit to reward the dog. Then transfer this sit signal that you have developed and use it when the dog is at your side. Reward in the same manner.

Other Heel Work Problems

We could go on for ever with the variation of problems that can occur in heel work and any other exercise for that matter, but the secret behind having few faults is good constructive training techniques, coupled with reliable motivation tools, patience, and the ability to reward what is right, when it is right, so that the dog can understand the connection. You must resist the temptation to use training sessions as workouts on completed exercises, and condition yourself into using them for good quality training time.

Circuit Training

Circuit training sounds rather tiring! But in fact it is designed to prevent you and your dog from getting bored, not particularly to keep you 100% fit, although it will help. The idea of circuit training is to set out as many obstacles as you can at your training session, these need not be heavy cumbersome obstacles, you could use bollards, markers, hoops, tapes on the ground, mini hurdles (these can be just a piece of dowel or cane between the

bollards). Obviously if you are lucky enough to have a large garden or training area of your own, then you can be more adventurous. You also need four or six ring posts and some cord to set up a ring. The ring posts do not need to be heavy duty, they can be the plastic poles that many handlers use for sendaways, weaving, or tracking markers.

When you go out training construct a ring and then place the obstacles in any order around the ring. Leaving some areas clear and others with a number of distractions. You can then commence to work around the obstacles. The object of the exercise is not to take a predictable course every time, but rather to twist and turn, working on keeping your complete concentration on the dog and his on you. You can use the cones to weave, the hoops to circle, etc., anything you like, but the important thing to remember is to keep the dog's complete and utter attention. Use your toy or *'want'* aid to make sure that the dog really wants to be with you. Don't become predictable. For instance, in the middle of a weave you can turn out and go in a different direction, or you could circle one of the bollards instead of weaving. The secret is to be inventive. This type of training is not just for the more advanced dogs, it can be introduced at any time. Obviously with a relatively untrained dog you will not be able to do any precision work, but you can play and work on *'the want'* amongst distractions and all of this will help you to keep your dogs full attention in all circumstances. The circuit also serves to prevent you from becoming staid or boring in your training. It stops you from marching up and down in a set pattern displaying to your dog just how boring heel work can be. The hurdle can be used whether you need it for your particular kind of obedience or not. It is there to give variety and help you to practice your control. Don't forget that in this as in all training, the most important thing is to read your dog. *Don't* carry on too long so that he becomes tired or bored. *Do* use your *'want'* aids, i.e. toy, ball and play. Use them in the same way that you would use them in teaching any other exercise, by giving and taking and keeping control of the game. During the course of the circuit you can go through all of your set exercises, (in a training manner of course, not as the finished article). Variety is the name of the game, keeping a 'high interest level' for both you and your dog.

If you are training with other people you can use each other to get the dogs used to working in close proximity, just as they might have to in the ring. A particularly good idea is to have one dog and handler working on either side of the ring ropes this often happens in competition but is rarely trained for. Another favourite with judges is to work you up to the ring ropes, to an obstacle, table or the like and then halt or turn. Use your circuit to prepare for this.

Remember the first rule, 'You must be the most interesting person to the dog'. Do not threaten or chastise your dog into watching or paying attention, this will only serve to make him more anxious to look away or in fact *get away* from this horrible person! You must teach the dog that you are nice, and singularly the most interesting person he knows, even if this means abandoning your more formal training and having a good rough and tumble or game of catch with him. Remember that your fun and games must be kept in close proximity to you. Don't get into the habit of letting the dog hurtle half way down the field after his ball. If you allow this all it tells the dog is that pleasure comes when he's away from you, all he gets when he's with you is boring repetition.

Once you have the dog's full attention and have achieved *'the want'*, then you can go back into a few steps of heel work whilst you have his full attention, thus getting perfection and full attention even with distractions. Even if you consider that what you get from your dog at this stage is far from perfection, if you have full *'wanting'* attention then perfection is just around the corner.

To recap, circuit training is not about a set routine. It is devised to keep you and your dog interested and keen, and to prevent you from becoming boring and repetitive. You might consider that you can do all of these variations without going to the trouble of carting obstacles and markers to the training area. When it comes to a real show you are rarely isolated with no distraction. I defy anyone to have the sort of memory that means that you know what comes next, and you certainly cannot decide for yourself what comes next! The obstacles will serve to help you to teach the dog that *you* are more interesting than anything around him, and also that obstacles which may be used as ring furniture are not frightening, nor something to be sniffed at or for leg cocking!

Recall to Present Position (Novice)

The Basis of a fast accurate recall

Before you start you should have a good bond with your dog and he should have achieved 'the want'. The first part of the recall can be moulded before you have any other formal part. The finer points can be introduced as the dog progresses, and after you have taught him to enjoy coming to you.

An important part of teaching a formal recall is teaching the dog to enjoy coming to you. If you are too formal and regimental every time, the dog soon becomes bored or turned off by the precision. It is good to vary your methods, each one being enjoyable for the dog.

Step one - Whilst walking your dog on lead allow him a little distance. Then when he is not necessarily expecting it, run backwards calling the dog. Make a great fuss when he gets to you, don't bother with placing him into the present position, just play or use food as reward. If you are training an older dog you may feel that this is a very basic start to the recall, but it will be useful in keeping up enthusiasm and instant control.

Step one can then be done in the presence of other dogs to make sure that the dog is happy to come to you, even when he is distracted by his canine pals. Obviously you may have to guide the dog or give a playful tug on the lead to get his attention and/or to start him coming towards you, but as he turns to you he must see pleasure, a warm friendly face, welcome arms and toy or titbit, *'Smudgie COME, Good Boy, Superman, COME'*. Emphasise the keyword *'COME'*, do not put any threat or aggression into your voice, make it clear and precise as if you were teaching a toddler a new word.

Step two - Once you are confident of success you can then progress to 'off lead' training in safe areas, and longer lines in more distractive circumstances. Be sure, if you release the dog, that you can get him back, don't risk failure.

Step three - The next thing you can teach the dog are the two hand positions. Hands together in front of you or held by your sides will mean present. Arms outstretched will mean come and play. In Beginner and Novice you can use this play signal to motivate the dog into a fast recall and then bring your hands together into the present position as he is on his way. The faster the dog the sooner you need to alter your hand position obviously. Don't change the signal when the dog is in full flight towards you too often without doing lots of genuine play signals resulting in play and cuddles. Other wise the signal will cease to mean play to the dog. It is like the one armed bandit fruit machine, if it doesn't pay out often enough it soon gets boring.

Step four - Don't allow yourself to become boring, vary your reactions. Sometimes you can call the dog and just before he reaches you start running away, and encourage him to come with you, have a game or just go racing with him. All of these things help to keep up the motivation level. Get a friend to hold your dog whilst you run away a fair distance, then as they release call the dog and make a great fuss.

Step five - Get a friend to hold your dog, walk away and leave him 20 feet or so and then call. As he comes towards you throw his toy through between your legs and beyond you, or simply about turn and throw, calling him back as soon as he picks up the toy. If the dog is familiar with your friend you can even have him running between the two of you. A great game for both handlers and dog.

Work on motivation using the momentum of the game to excite the dog. This will only serve a purpose if the dog is keen to come back with the toy, don't use this if your dog has a tendency to clear off with his toy. Start off on the lead. See the chapters on play and play training to learn how to control your dog's game

Flash is ultra keen to get to Sheila and the ball in this play recall

Preparing for the ring

The novice recall should be taught in separate parts. It is basically made up of three key word sections *SIT, PRESENT (COME), FINISH (CLOSE)*. Each of these key words are dealt with in their relative sections. The recall simply requires you to put them together in sequence. If you have taught the key words and there relative actions to your dog correctly, then, even if you have never put it together before you could go into a competition ring and perform a perfect recall. I know this through experience, the first time I worked my Border Collie, Leo, in the ring I had never put these elements together formally, and yet his recall was excellent. It is a better idea however, to link sections of the recall together at times, *(see Linking)* so that the dog learns to flow without anticipation.

It is *not* a good idea to continually practice a complete formal recall as your dog will inevitably develop inaccuracies. It is better to include all of the basic elements in your daily routine, only completing the exercise say once or twice a week. It *is* a good idea however to train with a friend and accustom the dog to hearing the sort of things that the ring steward will say like *'Leave your dog', 'Call your dog', 'Finish',* etc. This is not just for you to follow the instruction, although this will help you to become accustomed to the ring procedures, but so that the dog learns that he listens to you for the signal *not* the ring steward, so most of the time you will train against what is said.

So the sections to read for your perfect novice recall are: **presents, sits, close, and finish.**

Recall to the Heel Position (Test 'A' Recall)

Before you start the dog should understand the 'Heel position', 'Sit or 'Down', 'Close, 'Watch', be well motivated and have the 'Want'.

We will use this same principle of training for teaching the recall to the heel position, for the **'B'** and **'C'** test recalls from the sendaway.

The recall to heel is fairly self-explanatory. The dog is left in either the sit or the down. The handler leaves the dog as directed by the judge. In test 'A' the handler will call the dog using command signal or both whilst continuing to walk away from him. In test 'B' and 'C', the recall will follow the send away exercise. The handler may be walking in any direction when the dog is called by command or signal, (but not both). The dog will be expected to join the handler quickly and smoothly, and work in the correct heel position, continuing as directed by the judge or steward.

The exercise can be taught with the dog in the sit or the down position. My personal preference is the down position for a combination of reasons. Firstly, most dogs are more settled in the down, and later the exercise will be done with the dog in a down following the sendaway exercise. Starting this exercise in the down also gives the dog a clear differentiation from the novice recall, (recall the dog to the front present position), this is helpful when dog or handler are new to training.

Before you start be sure that the dog is stable and confident in your chosen position, sit or down. If he shows any confusion or apprehension go back to the **Stays** section for teaching of the static position before moving on to teaching the recall.

Step one - As usual the training begins on lead. Put the dog in position. *'Down'.* Take time to ensure that the dog is happy and confident. Hold your lead in your right hand. Remind him calmly *'Down'* before and as you take a forward step away from the dog, keeping your back to him. Run your left hand down the lead towards the collar ready to guide the dog. Then with friendly positive encouragement turn you head to the dog, looking over your left shoulder, give the dog your key word for heel work, *'Close'.* Use your left hand on the lead to guide the dog into the correct position. Walk a few paces with the dog in the heel work position remembering to keep your body posture upright, and your attitude friendly. Then break and play. Do not be too formal at this stage. Repeat this stage until the dog is confident and coming into position with accuracy and a minimum of help.

Step two - The next stage is to build up a little distance before calling the dog, very gradually literally a step at a time.   As you build up the exercise you can join two leads together, use a longer line or extending lead, to give more distance and yet remain in control, reeling the lead in to help the dog to take up a good heel position. Make sure that the equipment that you use is easily controlled, and that you are not struggling with yards of lead. If you do get muddled simply stop and play with the dog and then start again having gained control.

Step four - Once you have perfected a straight recall of about two lead lengths, then introduce a turn so that the dog learns to come into the heel position whilst you are horizontal to him. Go back to being only a pace away from the dog and have a single lead, but this time turn to your left in front of the dog. Call him using your key word *'Close'*, and at the same time step back with your right leg (or left if

Piper is a very keen dog and he is more easily controlled from the sit position, choose which position is best for you and your dog.

you lead with your right foot on left turns in heel work. See left turns). Run your left hand down the lead towards the collar and sweep the lead back, just as you would for a left turn in heel work. Guide the dog in to the heel position neatly. Take a few paces forwards with the dog in the heel position and then break and play.   Don' t be tempted to formalise and put in sits at the end, we will teach sits later and separately. Don't loose sight of what you are teaching. Have patience perfecting this stage keeping up the motivation level to be sure of a neat pick up. Don't be tempted to rush ahead just because you have had a successful straight recall. Good ground work now will save heartache and confusion later.

Step five - This time take an extra step forward before turning to put in a little more distance. Then proceed as above.   Once again use your lead to sweep the dog back and then into the heel position to teach a neat, tight pickup. Build up to a

Recall to Heel

lead's length or two as before, making sure that you have control all the time, but do not progress at the expense of enthusiasm, keep it fun.

Step six - Next teach the right handed pickup, this is not quite so easy as the dog has to come around you to the heel position, but take your time and be positive in your actions. Once again leave your dog in a confident down. This time you will leave the dog a couple of steps and turn right, remind the dog *'Down'* as you leave him. Hold your lead in your right hand and use your left hand as before to guide him in, turn and show him your toy or titbit to encourage him around you. Run your left hand down the lead to the dog's collar, gathering the lead up as he comes towards you. Guide the dog close in to the heel position using the heel work key word *'Close'*. Take a few steps forward to keep the momentum. Again build the exercise up slowly, taking time to make sure your have a good heel position and a neat, tight pick up without any surging or banging.

Teaching these turns is very similar to teaching the turns for heel work, and you will find that the training for one will aid the other. Use these starting blocks to gain the dog's confidence in the exercise. Keep it fun and light yet control for precision. If the dog anticipates do not chastise him. Simply call him in to position and then go back to the static position and train him in the down without calling him. If you chastise the dog you are putting in anxiety and confusion at best, and at worst a reluctance to do the exercise. You must remember not to get cross when the dog is actually doing what you are trying to teach him, albeit a little too soon for your liking. It does not make sense to be angry although we see people doing it all the time. Remember you are too late if you give chastisement after the event, even fractions of a second after, *even* fractions after the *start* of the event which may be *still* in action. *(See Timing)*. If things go wrong simply go back and spend more time on the static part of the exercise. Put enthusiasm and enjoyment into that part and not threat. Reward the dog for the correct behaviour ignore and restart when he goes wrong. Aim at making incorrect behaviour boring and meaningless by putting all of the emphasis and fun on the correct behaviour.

Step seven - After you have mastered the basic control training there are some exercises that will help build up confidence and style. Leave the dog in the down position go to the end of your longer lead and to the left a few paces, then simultaneously call the dog and start walking backwards. When the dog reaches your leg start walking forward and guide him in. Once the dog is happy doing this pick up to the left try turning to the right and repeating the process. This helps the dog to adjust his position on pickups, and can actually be used solely as the teaching method for the recall to the heel position.

Step eight - Another useful exercise is to leave the dog in the down, still holding the lead and turn left, right etc. and say the commands for example *'Right Turn, Left Turn, Halt, Call your dog'*, to accustom the dog to you turning as directed by the steward. Returning to the dog and rewarding him whilst he stays in the static position. When you first start this you may need a friend or a tape recording to call whilst you reassure the dog of the down position. If you already have problems then you definitely need to concentrate on the dog, reassuring him all of the time.

Trouble shooting

Beware that you don't repeat the exercise too much in one session as the dog will start to anticipate and come before you call him. Ideally be unpredictable as to whether you call him or not. Set up the exercise and call him, and then repeat, but this time reward him for staying down. Anticipation can also be caused by too much ring work or mock ring work and not enough training. The dog soon becomes accustomed to recall when he hears someone say, *'Call your dog'*. If you do do mock ring work, then make sure you train at the same time. If you set up a ring make it appear like a show, but train.

If your dog is reluctant to come or is easily distracted then you need to spend more time and enthusiasm in calling and rewarding. Be exciting, get out a toy or a titbit as the dog comes into position. Or as the dog comes toward you, throw his favourite toy ahead and slightly to the right of you. If he has a tendency to come in wide throw the toy across you well to the right hand side to encourage and motivate the dog in close to you, let him follow and collect the toy. This of course means the dog is not actually doing the excercise, but he is coming in to the correct direction and learning that it is fun. Do not formalise the exercise. Alternate precision and play, so one begins to be part of the other.

It is not necessary indeed it is pointless, to repeat the finished exercise over and over once the dog can do it, save the masterpiece for the ring. Faults should not creep in unless you end up doing more ring work than training, show off to often, or leave the dog to complete the exercise without the training aids.

Preparing for the ring

To prepare the exercise for the ring, gradually alternate the use of commands, reward, incentive and encouragement, as described in the section on *eliminating commands*. Ultimately you are allowed command and signal only in test 'A', and command or signal only in test 'B' and 'C' together with the dog's name. Your dog will have become accustomed to you turning your head in training to call him in to position. This head signal can be used in conjunction with his name in the ring. The head signal is a great signal to use for both you and the dog because;

a) It means you can *see* that the dog has heard and responded.

b) It directs your voice towards the dog. This is very important if you have a light voice or the wind is strong and in the wrong direction.

c) It is a friendly invitation to the dog, he will respond to your expression and this will help him to get it right.

Work on the static down. Set up situations so that you can teach the dog that you may walk, around and stewards may call, but it is nothing to worry about. Although we do not want the dog to fall asleep while he waits for you, he needs to be confident and unruffled by any external disturbances.

When any fault occurs go back to the drawing board, i.e. start from scratch. It won't take long, and will save a lot of anguish. Correction always shows itself in the ring, the dog who is taught by correction is normally disjointed and erratic in his work and so marked down by the judge accordingly.

Presents

'Present' should mean to the dog that he comes and sits in a straight position immediately in front of you, with his head held up watching and waiting for the next signal. Around the shows and training halls we can hear a varied deluge of 'verbal diarrhoea' for this quite simple exercise. 'Come, straight, front, present, get in, oy, not there, here', and many, many more together with the 'St Vitus Dance' style body language - no wonder dogs get so confused! It is better and far simpler for both dog and handler to use one simple key word coupled with hand positioning, to show the dog where you want him. The hand position is a useful signal because when you come to work without commands in the higher classes the hand position will act as a trigger in the dog's brain to guide him correctly. When he looks at you he will have the conditioned response and immediately knows what to do next. *(See Understanding).*

The simplest key word is the dog's name and the word *'Come'*. The hand position tells the dog whether to jump into your arms and have a cuddle and a game, (open and inviting arms), or to 'present' in front of you, (hands positioned in front of your body).

Yvonne Hollyoak using a low hand position for her Pyrenean Sheepdog, Holly.

Step one - At the outset we play games during which the dog is called with open arms and given lots of cuddles and a rough and tumble play. As always the game is on lead, down at dog level, and the *'want'* aid is used. The dog starts to associate the key word *'Come'*, with lots of fuss and open arms, and will soon be hurtling to you when he hears the word.

117

Step two - The next stage is to incorporate into the above game, some guidance of the dog into the correct present position. So play with your dog and when you are ready and feel in control, gather up the lead, simultaneously giving his name and key word, bring your hands together, flat on your stomach, and then reach down with one hand on the dog's rump and make sure the dog sits squarely in the correct position. Bring your hands back together, guiding his head up as you go, all the time try to keep your body posture as up right as possible. Pretty soon you will be able to manoeuvre the dog so that he comes into the correct position without the need to reach over. Make sure you always place your hands clearly and in a central position on your body, so that the dog has something to aim for. You may find it easier to use your toy or a titbit to give him incentive to *'present'* in the correct place.

Ronnie Jones uses a totally different position to Yvonne, adjusting to her dog's size

Technique Two

Another technique is to guide the dog in by slipping your hands through his collar at the front, and gently guiding him into place. The upward movement of your hands in the collar gently tilting him back into the sit position. Not all dogs respond quite so easily to this, particularly if they have been used to the pull of the collar meaning chastisement, but it is a very quick, and accurate method if your dog is responsive and happy with it. **Read Your Dog.**

Step three - Once your dog is happily coming into the *'present'* position, don't become totally formal . Keep the speed and *'Want'* up by doing lots of play recalls with open arms.

Step four - You can now go on to teaching the dog to come into the *'present'* from various angles. This reinforces the understanding of what is meant by the key word *'Come'*, and the hand signal to *'present'*. To start this, leave the dog in the sit position, stand slightly to the side but facing your dog at lead's length. Place the leg nearest to the dog out a little, so that the dog has to come around it to come in straight, this helps to bring him into the correct position. Call him in gathering in the lead and bringing your hands to the *'present'* signal position. Be ready to help every step of the way. Remember that the training procedure should be done in just as an exuberant fashion as the play, to attain good keen responses your dog should not know any difference between work and play. When the dog completes the position, finish as usual with your release word and play. As the dog grows more proficient you can make the angles more acute, but remember start each training session with the basics, to make sure your dog is on the right wave length. Occasionally the dog will respond better starting at more acute angles, there being a much bigger difference for him to home in on. Experiment and see which works best for you.

Presenting with a Retrieve or Scent Article

Presenting with an article should not be a problem if you have taught the above with careful step by step patience, guidance and fun. The dog may not realise that you require the same thing, (i.e. the present to front) to start with, so it is best to go through the basics of the present, (once he has learnt to retrieve), allowing the dog to happily hold the article in his mouth. If you have done your job properly with his *'Want'* toy, you may be able to show him what is required using this. Do not at any time put any mental or physical pressure on the dog that might result in him loosing confidence in you or his toy.

Finishes

Before you start - The dog should understand the key words 'Sit', 'Close', 'Good boy', and have 'The Want'.

The object of the exercise is to send the dog from the *'present'* position, to the heel position, with the dog ending up in a neat sit. It should be performed quickly, and the dog should not take a wide, erratic or distracted berth around the handler.

Teaching finishes is generally either neglected or over done. Currently in the ring the left handed finish seems to be the preferred discipline particularly with the more successful handlers. The usual reason given is that the dog can be seen all of the time, and the handler does not have to worry what is going on behind.

Teaching is relatively simple follow the stages. Some of the stages will need to be progressed over several training sessions, unless the dog is already well versed and mature. Don't expect to get perfection in one go.

Teaching the left handed finish

Piper's motivator is his lead so it never goes out of sight making him superbly keen

Step one - Get the dog in the correct frame of mind, i.e. create *'The Want'*. Put him in the sit position in front of you, tell him *'Sit'*. Go to the end of your lead, hold your lead and your toy in your right hand, and place your right hand in the present signal position, and keep it there as much as possible *(see presents.)* Use your left hand to run down the lead towards the dog's collar. Step back with your left leg and call the dog using his heel work word *'Close'*. Continue walking backwards to create the backwards flow, using your left hand to guide the dog back into the heel position and preventing him from jumping, until you have his head coming into your leg. Then take a few steps forward to bring the dog into the correct position. Place him in the straight sit position. Reward him in the position and then release.

Step two - When the dog is able to understand the above, and is performing with enthusiasm, you will gradually be able to take less steps back. Work on this until the only leg movement is the left leg taking one step back and then coming back to join your right.

Step three - Now we will start to get closer to the dog. Gradually shortening the length of lead, until we can stand immediately in front of the dog and simply step back with the left leg and guide with the left hand.

Step four - The step back can now be shortened to make it less obvious but if the dog is unsure widen your step when he needs it. Try to start off each time with both hands in the present position, because this is what the dog will eventually see.

Step five - The left hand down the lead can now be brought to a minimum, but continue to use it as the signal. This way the hand is always going in the right direction if the dog needs help. Again try to start off with both hands in the present position.

Step six - Vary your aids, sometimes step back, sometimes use your lead. Introduce turns following the finish so that the dog does not start to assume that he will be released at the end.

Teaching the right handed finish

The Right handed finish is often favoured by handlers of larger more cumbersome breeds. It does not require such a tight turn, and the dog can whip around with ease if sufficiently motivated.

Step one - Get the dog in working mode i.e. achieve *'The want'*. Put him in the sit position in front of you. You can remain fairly close, hold your lead in your right hand, fairly close to the dog's collar, tell the dog *'Close'*, as you step back with your right leg, taking as many steps as necessary to get the dog on his feet and on

Finishes

his way past you on your right. When the dog reaches your side start walking forwards so that the natural momentum makes the dog move around you, transfer the lead into the left hand and bring the dog around into the sit position beside you.

If you feel that you are getting in a taffle with your lead, you can pass it behind you and into your left hand before you start. Then just reel it in as the dog comes into position.

Step two - The obvious progression is to gradually take less steps, before bringing the dog around, and after he comes into position. The more you motivate him the quicker this will come. This can become a very boring exercise so make sure that you keep it exciting and light. If the dog is slow coming around use your toy to motivate him, do not place him in the sit, instead just throw the toy as he comes around, and let him go forward for it. You can soon introduce the sit to a motivated dog, it is more difficult to speed up a switched off dog. Make sure that the dog is remaining tight behind you, keep the lead tight so that there is no room for manoeuvre.

Step three - As the movement on your part is reduced, the hand to the right can become the signal to the dog. It will therefore always be there to help if necessary. If your dog is particularly large or quick in his movement, you will find it useful at least to start with to position yourself near a wall or in a corner, so that when he comes into the heel position the wall prevents him from going wide.

Caution - once you have perfected the finish do not tag it on to every relevant exercise, if you do the dog will soon start to anticipate and/or loose the sparkle. Keep him guessing!

122

Leave on Command

*Before you start - The dog need **not** know any formal exercises, although an understanding of what is meant by 'Sit', will be a useful tool to help keep him under control and make him focus on the job in hand. He must however, be confident in his handler.*

This exercise, although it is not a formal obedience test exercise, is a very useful discipline to teach your dog. It will be used to tell the dog to leave other dog's, to ignore incorrect articles, leave people alone, keep off furniture, and has all manner of other applications within the competition world and at home. Use it when you need it and taught as a proper exercise it will serve you well.

Step one - Put the dog in a sit or have him otherwise under control on his lead. Take a titbit, or part of his dinner. Give him a small piece so that he gets a taste. Take another piece and show him what you have, he will assume that it is for him so this time as he reaches forwards, say the key word *'Leave',* in an authoritative yet pleasant manner, and prevent him from getting the titbit by using your lead to pull him back away from the treat. It may be a bit of struggle to start with and the dog may be puzzled by your actions, but persevere in a pleasant and controlled manner, until he sits back away from the treat. As soon as he does this, reward him with the treat, but introduce a key word to say that he may have it, *'Take it'.*

Daniel teaches Spotty to Leave controlling the dog with the lead.

123

Leave on Command

Step two - Repeat as above, this time the dog may start to get the message. If he sits back and pulls away from the treat straight away, go immediately in with the reward. This is the behaviour you are striving for so reward it. If he tries to get to the treat, pull him back, and keep him there a few seconds, and then reward, *'Take it'.*

Step three - Repeat again, by now most dogs are starting to understand. As you approach with the treat, tell him *'Leave'*, count a few seconds and then reward him, *'Take it'.*

Step four - Build up the length of time that the dog is sitting or withdrawing from the titbit. If he does really well reward him sooner. The rewards now can start to come at various, unpredictable times. Count to yourself to see how you and the dog are improving. 1,2,3,4, *'Take it'.* 1,2,3,4,5,6, 'Take it', and so on.

Step five - Now you can transfer the dog's new found control to differing circumstances and objects. Choose an object in the house that the dog is not to have, control him whilst you wave it in front of him. Give him the key word *'Leave'*, when he pulls back away from the object, reward him with a treat.

This can be broadened into all sorts of situations. The dog can be taught not to jump up, not to go on furniture, to keep away from the gate, all using the same basic procedure, simply adjusting for each situation, and controlling the dog so that he knows what you do or do not want.

Retrieve

*The minimum that your dog should understand before you start: The 'Want', 'Play', the key word 'Come'. The minimum **you** should understand before you start: Timing, bonding, the dog's mind, the objective of the exercise.*

The interpretation of the rules into normal day to day language tells us that we require the dog to remain sitting still and quietly in the heel position until sent for the article on the command or signal of the handler. The dog must make a natural, positive, straight out run, a neat clean pick up of the article, a brisk, unhesitant, straight return to the centre front of the handler, sit squarely in a neat centrally accurate position in perfect line with the handler, hold the article until the handler reaches and takes it, go to the heel position on handler's signal or command. The article must at all times, during the period that is held by the dog, be carried positively without chewing, rolling or otherwise mouthing. The dog should perform this task, as all others in a *'happy natural manner'.*

Retrieve is one of the major stumbling blocks for handlers in competitive obedience. Such a natural instinctive exercise should really pose very few problems, but it does. Most puppies quite naturally retrieve, the problems normally start to creep in when any form of precision is introduced by the trainer.

If you read and understand the chapter within the concepts section which covers the understanding of the dog's mind, you will realise what a complex task you are asking the dog to undertake. Such precision and accuracy can only be achieved and maintained if the dog understands, and is motivated to enjoy every tiny component of the exercise. To achieve this we must break down the task into fragments.

Most of you will have achieved with your dog some form of play retrieve. If your dog does not like to play, this is dealt with in the concepts section under *'play training'.* The play retrieve is a very useful motivator to use in conjunction with teaching a more formal retrieve. It also serves to help the dog differentiate between the two, as the handler should use a different key word for each. *'Hold'* for formal retrieve for instance, and *'fetch it'* for play retrieve. The actual words that you choose don't matter, use what ever you feel comfortable with but be consistent and think about what you are saying and doing.

It will be of great benefit if you have effectively taught your dog the meaning of the key word *'come'.* If the dog is instantly and happily able to respond to this word then it will avoid any jerking on the lead which could mean that the dog drops the article. Put yourself in the dogs shoes; you trot out to get the article, just as you have your mouth around it some idiot, (sorry, handler!), jerks your neck off and yells *'come'.* Whether this is done in a pleasant manner or not, you are going to stop what you are doing and respond, either enthusiastically, apologetically or begrudgingly depending on your handler's attitude. You will assume from the signal, that the handler no longer wants you to collect the article but instead he wants you to come straight back.

If your dog has not learnt the controlled *'sit'* don't worry, you don't need it to start with. You can introduce the control and sit part of the exercise when it has been successfully taught as a separate exercise. Likewise the *'present'* and *'finish'.* Don't loose sight of what you are teaching at each stage, be sure that the dog has had a thorough grounding in each component before attempting to put things together.

You must decide on the key words that you intend to use. Find a suitable article for the dog to learn the exercise on, and have a clear mental picture of the exercise. The article that you choose should be comfortable for the dog. If you decide that you would like to start with a dumb-bell, then it is a good idea to wrap some thick, soft cloth around it, towelling is ideal. This is particularly important if you are training a puppy, a soft mouthed dog, or if you have a dog which has had bad experiences in the past. A wider diameter mouth piece is less likely to be moved around in the mouth, and so will be easier for you to prevent the mistakes of chewing etc. With puppies it is best to wait until they are through the teething stage before you put in any serious work, but informal preparation is covered in the section on preparing your puppy for a career in competitive obedience.

Timing *(see concepts section)*, is a crucial element in teaching a good and reliable retrieve. If your timing is not spot on you could end up achieving the opposite to your wishes! I like to practice my timing without the dog just as you might perfect footwork without the dog. Pretend your left hand is the dog's mouth, open it place your article in it, tell it 'Hold, good boy', take it and keep quiet. Get used to placing, taking, praising, and using key words at the correct time, before you go on to the real thing - the dog!

Most dogs prefer to retrieve a moving target. Being of a predatory nature, it is in their basic make up to hunt. In the absence of hunger to drive them, they will enjoy practising the skill of the chase. This is the part of their instinctive behaviour that we are about to modify.

So let us start..........

Step one - Have you dog on lead and a comfortable non restrictive collar. Start with your dog on your left if you can although this is not crucial. Take your article in your right hand and entice the dog to take hold of it by waving it around along the floor or in front of him just beyond his reach. Once he is stimulated by it allow him to go forward to take it, praise him, *'Good boy'*, and then take the article before he has time to move it around in his mouth, or wonder what he is supposed to do next. Repeat this a couple of times, and then go on to something else at the first training session.

Step two - Repeat as step one when the dog is confident in taking the article introduce the turn towards you by calling him using your key word *'Come'*, gently guide him with the lead collecting it up as he comes towards you and then take the article from his mouth. Don't yank the lead as the dog may think that you want him to drop the article. The amount of time that the article is in the dog's mouth should be minimal, seconds only, not allowing time for the dog to start any chewing.

Step three - Once you get the feel of this you can introduce the key word *'hold'*. I find that to start with it is best to say nothing to the dog except maybe to make a few exciting sounds to motivate him to make a move toward the article, *'Ready, steady!'.* When you have got used to the speed and

Once the dog is confident a little more formality can be introduced.

movement of your dog introduce the word 'hold' as he goes towards and takes the article. Remember that this is the first stage of what you are trying to achieve, i.e. *'hold'* means go out, pick up and bring back. Your voice should not sound threatening at any time *'hold'* should be fun, and it should sound the same as it will in the ring when the master piece is complete. You should be very appreciative and encouraging to the dog at the time that he is doing what you want, that is, going forward and taking the article. Once the article has been taken from the dog's mouth immediate calm and quiet is necessary. Do not carry on praising, remember the dog cannot associate praise for a job which has been done, only to what is happening at the time of the reward. If you carry on praising after you have taken the article the dog will often start to throw the article at you or even refuse to pick articles up in the future, associating praise at the end of the exercise as the thing that he is rewarded for. It is human nature to praise after the event, in a *'Good dog - well done'* manner, but we must learn to think like a dog if we want to be successful at training.

Step four - So now you have the dog happily going towards the article collecting it from your extended hand and returning to you. Once you have perfected the above stages you can start to work on other components of the exercise to introduce the precision. Depending on the type of dog sometimes I now introduce the control element i.e. the sit prior to going out. This is normally the next stage for a very attentive and keen dog. Sometimes I begin progressively to get the article nearer and nearer to the ground no more than a few inches at a time, and going only as fast as the dog remains confident. Sometimes I combine the two. You must read your dog and aim for and achieve success all of the time. When you do get to the stage where you have the article to the floor, keep

Soon the dog will be reaching forward to hold the article in a more controlled manner.

your hand underneath it and then the next stage is to have your hand just by it to give the dog confidence and help to make the progression more positive. Don't jump the stages from holding it near the floor to standing back and sending the dog because either he won't understand what you mean or you will be allowing the dog too many chances to go wrong. Either way problems will occur.

Retrieve

Step six - When you feel the dog is very confident in picking up the article and coming back, and having taught the present as a separate exercise *(see Present),* you can begin to introduce the present into the retrieve exercise, linking the two components together. Collect up the lead and bring your hands together into the present position signal as the dog comes towards you. Guide him with your lead keeping it under his chin. To start with you may not be able to get a perfect present, do not loose the retrieve in favour of the present, simply guide the dog and step by step get nearer to what you want. Reward when the dog is correct ignore when wrong. Keep your reward, toy or titbit high and central on your body to help the dog to aim for a good present, if he looks up to you as he approaches his body flows naturally straight. Sometimes you can hold the reward under your chin. This leaves your hands free, and also mean that the reward is in full view, and central for the dog to aim at. If you have a very lively dog this might prove a little hazardous for you, i.e. the dog may catch your face if he jumps towards his toy in excitement, so only do it if your are sure of your dog.

Step seven - When the dog is happily collecting the article from your outstretched hand etc., then you can work on getting him to take it bringing your hand progressively closer to the dog, so that eventually it is immediately in front of him. Working back to this stage will help him to understand more fully the concept of the key word *'Hold'*. By the time you are at this stage the dog should be automatically turning and coming into the present position with only a modicum of help and guidance. Remember to keep the time that he has the article in his mouth to an absolute minimum and not to put the dog under pressure.

Step eight - Start to increase the time that the dog has the article in his mouth only when he displays a confident and accurate attitude to the job in hand. Then the time should be extended by only fractions of seconds each time. Never put any pressure on the dog as an anxious dog will be the first to mouth. Think about yourself, if you are nervous, anxious or simply excited your mouth goes dry and you lick your lips, if you have something in your mouth this is not so easy, so you try to adjust the thing in your mouth to make yourself more comfortable. In obedience we call this *'mouthing'.* From an animals point of view it is very difficult to control, particularly when you do not posses the brain power to understand the reason or cause. So we humans must use our brain power to achieve the results that we want, and realise what is going on within the dog's body which is beyond his control.

Step nine -   Now the dog is beginning to be competent it is time to introduce other exercises which will have a beneficial effect on the end product.   Teaching the dog to go around the article to collect it can be a good idea to use with a fast dog because it avoids a pounce prior to pick up. This exercise is accomplished by holding your hand over the article and guiding the dog from your left hand side with the lead around the article which is placed a few feet away on the floor. The dog is guided and blocked so that he has to collect the article from the back when he is facing you. This is then progressed by placing your foot to the left of the article and guiding the dog around to pick up from the back. As the dog gets the hang of it you pull back your foot so that it is not quite in contact with the article as you send the dog, the dog will continue to work as if your foot was there, and of course you are ready to move in if the dog should show any signs of going wrong. Your movement can become progressively less but don't forget to do the basic exercise at each session so that the dog does not start to introduce his own variations on the theme!

Step ten - Once the dog is confident introduce many variations into training so as not to become predictable, and to keep the dog attentive and interested. If you continually throw the article and send your dog, (a trap that many fall into once the dog has mastered the basic exercise), the dog will become either bored or over keen and difficult to handle, and certainly mistakes will creep in all to quickly. Training should be controlled and varied. Build up routines always going through basic control steps at each training session and prior to going into the ring. Save the master piece for the very odd occasion to convince yourself that the training is working and, of course, for the ring.

Teaching the dog to pick up different articles

The same principles apply to the dog learning how to pick up different articles and different textures as are applied to the basic teaching. Everything should be taken step by step. The articles sometimes may need to be masked and introduced gradually in order for the dog to accept them. To give you an example of this, I had a dog who did not like to pick up cloth, in fact he positively hated it. He did however love his squeaky ball. After much head scratching, we decided that the best way to tackle the problem was to make a hole in the ball and stuff the cloth inside. At first the dog was not convinced even with this as he could associate the smell of the cloth although he could not see or feel it. So then we acquired another ball identical to the first and got him motivated on this. Whilst he was keen we swapped the toys over and he came in with the stuffed ball, mildly puzzled but happy enough. Immediately we reverted to the other ball and built his confidence back up, and then once again when he was ultra confident threw the stuffed ball. Each time he was sent for the stuffed ball he grew more and more confident. After separate sessions built up over a few days, we decided that the time was right and pulled a tiny corner of the cloth out from the ball. Again at first he was a little puzzled, but such was his confidence now that we were able to progressively pull out more and more until eventually he would retrieve the cloth and then the ball alternately, learning that the cloth was not so bad after all. Once he was confident we carefully introduced, a tiny step at a time, the precision. Always having the ball at hand to encourage and motivate him. Of course he understood the concept of the precision because we had done our ground work correctly in the first place, and so therefore he progressed in leaps and bounds. You can use this technique in a variety of ways with other articles, wrapping or tying articles with something more acceptable to the dog. Alternating confident articles with not so confident articles, building on confidence all of the time and then bringing in precision later.

Some dogs become excellent retrieve dogs but lack the courage or confidence to work away from the handler and so the technique of throwing toys alternated with retrieve articles will build up confidence for distance. Only do this once you know that the dog is accurate, or as a play exercise, not expecting precision, because when the dog is at a distance you are leaving him to his own devices. Do it to often and he will devise his own version of retrieve!

It is always a matter of striking the balance and reading your dog, confidence without assumption, accuracy and precision without boredom. If things keep going wrong don't sit back and watch, while the dog repeats the mistake time and time again, gradually loosing your temper or worse still becoming annoyed with the dog. Step in and alter the situation to guide the dog into the correct actions. Don't be frightened of mistakes we all make them.

'My dog won't pick up the article at all' Incentive Retrieve.

Many handlers will make mistakes along the way often resulting in the dog not wanting to participate in the retrieve exercise at all. Sometimes dogs are just not that interested, even though they will quite readily play. This is where one of the most important things in a dog's life comes into play 'FOOD'. Play is a building block in the natural process of learning how to get your food if you are a dog as you will have learnt in the introduction. So therefore food is a primary motivation. If your dog is food motivated then you can use this to teach him to retrieve. The same procedures can be followed as above but substitute the article for something that the dog can smell has food in it but will not be easily broken by the dog. For a soft mouthed dog a Smartie tube or bag tightly wrapped and enclosing treats will be suitable. If you have a dog with a harder bite then you may have to use a more solid tube or packet. The dog does not necessarily have to get his reward directly from the packet although if this can be arranged it works very well. As long as the dog can't take the food himself it will work. You will need to keep some of the same food in your hand to reward the dog. The stumbling block with this method comes if your timing, which is even more crucial here, goes wrong. You must aim to reward the dog very quickly as he brings in the article, but he must learn that *you* take the article and *then* he gets the reward. If you don't he will soon get into the habit of spitting it out at you in order to eat his treat. It is crucial that he soon starts to associate the Key word *'Hold'* with reward. The principle behind this is the same as building up time using the titbit reward in the controlled sit. The dog must learn to hold the position, or in this case the article in order to get the reward. This is done using the shaping technique   ignoring incorrect behaviour and rewarding correct behaviour building up his retrieve incentive a second at a time. As the dog progresses the rewards are given for that little bit more effort, to encourage when the dog is unsure or even for a small step forward. The dog soon starts to eliminate the behaviours which do not get the reward.   Once the dog is confident, transferring to other articles is the same as above. Take your time be patient and *you* will be rewarded.

No Force

I am not in favour of force methods of training, these are methods whereby the dog learns that in order to avoid the pain he must conform. With retrieve this is all too common. In the hands of a trainer who has perfect timing, forcing, although painful for the dog, can work. But, if that handler is so good I don't see that they need to revert to such methods which I'm sure they would not like to show to the general public. In the hands of a trainer who is not so accurate life can be absolute hell for the dog, to say nothing of the anguish that the handler goes through trying to perfect a sport that he is supposed to be enjoying.

In common with many people of my era, way back when I first started training I was told that the only way to be sure of a perfect retrieve was to force the dog so that he would never say no. With the knowledge of animal behaviour which I have gained and can now share with you, I'm sure you will agree with me that any method of teaching which inflicts pain mentally or physically is totally unnecessary and in some cases downright barbaric. Please, if you are just starting in this field, seek out instructors who do **not** use methods where by the dog has to perform to avoid the pain of the teaching techniques, and then those who have not got the dog's welfare at heart will have to change their ways or fall by the wayside.

Retrieve over a hurdle

Jumping a hurdle is a relatively easy task to teach a dog. Obviously we must wait until he is old enough and strong enough to take a full size hurdle, but even as a young dog we can be introducing him to a key word for instance each time he takes a jump over a small log in the park. Be observant use the environment and day to day life to aid your training.

Step one - When the dog is old enough and well developed physically, more formal training can start. Begin with a very low hurdle, say 6" from the ground and jump over with your dog. Keep him on lead of course, just walk briskly towards the jump and over.

Step two - Once you and the dog are happily going over, introduce your key word for jump, *'Over'*, the word should come in just as he is about to lift into the jump.

Step three - When the dog is happily doing this with you, you can try sending him. Don't just send the dog on his own, stand at the side of the jump with your head looking at the dog from the other side, throw his toy over to give him confidence and motivation to go without you, and then call his name, guide him with the lead, so the options to do anything other than jump are minimal. This normally sparks off a keen reaction. If the dog shows any apprehension, go over with him again and encourage him to collect his toy. If the dog tries to go around the hurdle to collect his toy, throw the toy over and go with him a few times to eliminate that behaviour. If your dog already knows the static sit position you can leave him in the sit, go over the jump yourself, and then call him over. You will have a hold of his lead to guide him and prevent him from going in the wrong direction. Remember praise and the key word must be given at the correct time. Praise him as he lifts and comes over not when he is over and by your side and the exercise is all but finished. The sequence should go like this: *'Tyke - Ready Ready , Over - Good boy'.* Work on this until the dog is confidently going over the jump and collecting his toy, on and off lead.

Step four - Now the dog is confident we must introduce the return. This should come relatively easy. Simply position yourself at the right hand side of the jump. Put the dog in the sit position facing the jump to your left. Throw the dog's toy over the jump, send him over to collect his toy, as he goes over the jump you

Retrieve

reposition yourself in front of the jump to call the dog as he turns with his toy. Use your lead to guide him back over the jump to you. You may find it advantageous to have another toy to encourage the dog back. A short cut to this is to teach the dog in an area where the only option to get back is over the jump. In a corridor for instance, or over a fence. This works very well as the basic teaching principle but you will need to use your lead to guide the dog the first time that you introduce a hurdle to make sure that he understands what you want.

Step five - Once the dog is doing the jump, retrieve and return, introduce the present. Again the dog should be on lead so that you can guide him where you want him. Don't expect that he will automatically know just because you may have taught it as a separate exercise. As soon as you introduce a variable like this the dog is likely to be confused. Follow the principle as for teaching presents, guiding him in to the correct position with your lead.

Step six - All this time you have been using a toy as the retrieve article, this is to give confidence. Now you can change to your dumb-bell or other article. Start on lead as you did at the start of teaching, helping the dog all of the way and never expecting too much, and working through all of the stages. By now the dog should be very confident, and if your normal retrieve training has been implanted correctly the dog will have no problem transferring to any article.

Stays

The teaching of stays is often a much neglected discipline. Generally some positive structured time is taken when the dog is a puppy but then, as he grows the tendency is to rush to get onto more interesting things like heel work, retrieve, etc., as soon as the dog is more mature.

The three static positions, *Sit, Down, and Stand* are the basis and control element of many of the teaching exercises, so it is of utmost importance that the dog is happy and confident in these positions, and truly understands the meanings of the three key words.

Some breeds and types of dogs are more prone to anxiety and/or have high instinctive drives that make them strive to keep the family together. These types are more likely to break stays than others. In a survey done by Obedience Competitor Magazine in Britain, more German Shepherd Dogs than any other breed broke the stay exercise at obedience shows. These were also the dogs most likely to mouth or even destroy retrieve and scent articles, another common trait of the anxious dog. One shouldn't feel defeated by this fact, all is not lost, but armed with this knowledge you should realise that great time and patience must be taken especially with this type.

The more anxious the dog, the more likely it is that he will want to break and come to find you or simply to run away panicking, causing chaos around the show ground. There is nothing more embarrassing or soul destroying than having your day spoilt by your dog running away when he is supposed to be working with you in the ring. There is nothing more frustrating than having your round spoilt by someone else's dog running riot, whilst you are working.

So we need to teach the dog the discipline in such a way that the dog will become stable, content and confident when we leave him. This means, as with all of your training that you must be patient, confident in your approach and thorough.

The Sit

Some methods will work better than others for teaching this position, much depends on you and your dog, and your experiences so far. If you have been spending much time getting the dog into the sit position as for DC, i.e. in front of you using a toy or titbit incentive, then the dog tries to avoid being in the sit position beside you and is more likely to want to sit to the front, or he may have a tendency to try to wriggle away when he hears the key word *'sit'*. If you have this problem allow the dog to sit in the position he has become accustomed to and then *you* move in to the side of *him*, stroke him and soothe him with your voice. When he is settled gently move away again. Build up the exercise as you would any other, a little at a time. Doing this will prevent him from becoming confused or feeling pressured. You may find that changing the key word and/or signals, including body stance for this control exercise will help if you have spent very much time on the DC type of sit before teaching the sit at your side. It is a fault that occurs more often amongst competitive handlers who are working on their second or third dog, because it is very enjoyable for the handler teaching the DC style positions, they can be introduced quite early, and practised just about anywhere. A favourite time for throwing them in is whilst watching TV or in between play retrieve sessions.

Sitting Puppies

If you are starting with a pup, then you need to come down to puppy level. Bob down by his side, gently encouraging and guiding him into position on your left. Have him on lead of course, hold the lead in your right hand and when you have the dog in the correct position place your left hand flat on his rump, your right hand is used to guide his head up, keep the lead positioned under his chin, hold it fairly short near to his chin and have a titbit or toy in the same hand to entice and then reward him as he comes into the correct position.

Once you have perfected your technique, and are able to co-ordinate properly, introduce the key word *'sit'* so that the dog can start to understand the connection. The right hand should be brought up above the dog's head so that his nose follows, then the natural progression is for his back end to make contact with the floor. If you are careful to do this in the same way each time, the hand position will become an added signal to the dog, this may be of use later on when handling the dog at a distance or in a noisy area.

When the dog is starting to become confident in the sit position gently adjust the lead position to the back of his neck to help to control him whilst *you* rise into a more erect position, keep helping him all the time and be ready the second he twitches in the wrong direction to make sure that he keeps in the sit. Anticipate any movement and learn to read his every breath, you must react before he goes wrong.

Do not try to keep the exercise going for too long at one go. Seconds of the correct procedure are far better than longer periods of struggling and or correction.

Coming down to dog level with a puppy or small dog can be a long way down!

Sitting Older dogs

Depending on the size of your dog it may be necessary for you to go down on one knee to guide the older dog into position using the same procedure as described for puppies. If you *have* a larger dog try to keep your back straight as you position the dog, i.e. your torso should be facing front, bend at the knees, and guide the dog into the sit position using your lead and hands as described above. Obviously you may have to turn towards the dog to start with, in order to gain control but you should aim to keep as straight as possible. You can use the titbit or toy to help, bringing it up in line with the dog's body to guide him straight.

Some very large dogs can be helped into the sit position by running your hand down the back of the hind legs, as you come to the knee joint and apply a little pressure, you will feel the dog start to bend forward into the sit position, encourage and give confidence as the dog may wonder what is happening to him to begin with. This technique works particularly well with breeds like Great Danes.

With long bodied dogs the use of a wall is an added bonus. Sometimes it is a virtual impossibility to reach the back end of the dog with your hand especially if he wants to swing away to the side in an effort to see your face. Position yourself and the dog so that the wall acts as a barrier, preventing him from going to the side. This is a good technique to use on heavy dogs, or for people who are not as strong as they would like to be, it takes away the strain on the handler, and gives you much more control.

The key word that I use for this exercise is *'Sit'*. I do not find it necessary to have differing words for the sit position in different exercises because I always ask the same kind of body movement from the dog, although for DC the word is said in an elongated fashion to make sure that I get it over the distance, often being a quietly spoken person I revert to the hand signal for distance control. The sit in the 'present' position (retrieve or recall) will be done on one commencing keyword only, that is the recall key word *'Come'*.

The Down Position

The down is a submissive position, and many dogs feel vulnerable when manipulated at the outset. If, when the position is first introduced to a mature dog (or even sometimes a puppy), he shows any awkwardness or aggression when you attempt to control him into the down, then you must think seriously about applying dominance control rules in the home as well as in training. If allowed to continue or the signs are ignored, dominance can become a major problem that may creep up on you unawares. *This is covered in my first book 'Everybody Can TRAIN Their Own Dog' (TFH), and more fully in my booklet 'Dominance in the Home', published by OCM.*

As with the sit, if you have been doing early DC training your dog may be a little confused to start with when you try to place him into the down position by your side although with the static down we will not be asking the dog to go into a sphinx position as we would for DC, rather he should be flat on his side or at least flopped over to one side on his haunches. The procedure should be followed as in the sit if he does show any confusion, i.e. *you* go to *his* side until he becomes more confident and accepts the change, the use of a different word will also help to quell confusion.

Puppies

Starting with a young pup is always the easiest because they are so pliable and simple to manage. Place your right hand at the front of the dog under and to the side of his chin. You may wish to slip your hand into the collar of larger or more powerful pups. For the smaller or less robust pup simply cup the dog around the shoulders, and with one hand on the dog's back simply slide him back and slightly sideways in to the down position. Have the lead attached to his collar just in case you lose control whilst trying to manipulate him into position. You can then get a hold of the end before the dog disappears, and encourage him back to you giving you the added bonus of retaining complete control. You shouldn't need to use the lead to get a small pup into position, kind, gentle hands can do all of the work.

To give the dog added incentive you can use a titbit or toy to entice him into position, but often it is not necessary if the dog has confidence in you, your own presence will be incentive enough for him to want to work with you. If you use a titbit it should come straight down between his two front paws, bringing it forward will result in the dog coming forward and probably into the stand position, or at least crawling forwards with his bottom in the air. Remember that the position that the dog finds himself in is what he will come to associate with the key word or signal used. If you are getting the wrong result simply alter your positioning until you can get the correct result. Make sure you have perfected your handling technique and then introduce the key word *'Down'* to teach him the connection of word and action. Once again your hand position pointing down towards the floor, together with your body stance will become a signal to use later if and when necessary.

Older dogs

Immature young adults often go through a wriggly stage where it becomes difficult to control them with your hands and the more you touch them the more wriggly they become. This is when you need to have a hands off approach to teaching, the use of your toy or titbit comes into play, bringing the motivator straight down between the dog's front paws as described above, and then, only when the dog is in position, do you introduce your hands to gently soothe him. You will probably have to build up any touching of the dog fairly gradually, a little at a time, teaching him that your hands don't automatically mean a rough and tumble game and that they can be very soothing.

Imagine the dog as if he were a roll of carpet. If you were to push straight down you would be unable to knock it over, but push to the side and it goes over easily. The same principle applies to your dog.

With larger dogs you should use their own weight to your advantage. One can learn a lot from watching martial arts experts, and the way in which they use weight and balance. Place your hand on the dog's shoulder and feel the direction of his push, if you apply gentle pressure, he will usually push back. You can learn to use this, in that you can release the pressure and pull the dog towards you and into the down. You must learn to get the timing just right and with practice you

139

will be able to apply this technique to the largest of dogs. When you know that you can get the procedure right introduce the key word *'Down'* and the dog will start to connect the word with the action.

There are very many techniques to help you to get the dog into the down position, even with older dogs the method described for puppies is a good one to start with, you may have to be a little stronger than you would with a pup but having said that it should not be a force type procedure, the dog should be simply manipulated with encouragement and kindness. It must be remembered that this is very submissive position for the dog to find himself in. He will feel vulnerable and may become a little distressed to start with. You must give him courage and confidence and create a calming effect with your attitude towards him. If you become irritated or angry he will worry that something is indeed wrong and will not settle easily, if at all!

All animals have nerves that send direct messages to the brain, rather like when the doctor tests your reflexes by hitting your knee with a little hammer. The dog has some reflexes that can be a useful aid to getting him into the down position. The dog must be relaxed in order to get a good result. Have him standing or sitting in front to you to start with and feel around the front of his chest for his breast bone. Gently move your hands around either side of the breast bone and you will find two small indentations. In this area are the pressure points and you will see various nerves twitching around the hind legs as you gently manipulate the area. If you are very patient and keep the dog relaxed you will eventually find the nerves that operate the muscles and make the dog go into the down position. The dog will slide gracefully down as you apply very gently pressure. He may be a little bewildered to begin with, but after a while you will come to know the correct position to touch your dog and he will soon be down. Once the dog has grown accustomed to you using this technique he will start to collapse into position as soon as he sees your hand coming towards him.

The key word that I use for the down is normally *'Flat'*, when teaching for a stay situation. For laying down in the house I use *'Settle'*, which is a command that means go down where you like.

The Stand

Of the three positions the stand is the most neglected. It is certainly always the one that I forget, and I have to condition myself into training it. My pupils will confirm that I nearly always forget to put it in when teaching stays in class and they have to remind me. As with the other two positions and excess DC training, this will make the dog a little confused to start with, but the training should be approached in the same way, moving into the dog's side and building confidence. If the dog is particularly body sensitive as many are when you attempt to bodily heave them into a stand position, a titbit is a useful aid to get them to their feet with a minimum of fuss and effort. The titbit should be held in your right hand marginally above nose height, (dog's nose that is)! Then move your hand and titbit gently, horizontally forward to bring the dog up into the stand position. If you hold the titbit too high the dog will just look up, or even try to come up on his hind legs, too low and he will go down. Trial and error will help you to get this right. Don't put in any key words until you have the procedure correct. Your left hand should contain your lead coupled up and held close to the dog's collar to make sure that the dog does not paddle too far forward. This of course will be further prevented if you make sure that you stop moving your right hand as soon as the dog is on its feet. If your right hand keeps moving the dog will keep following, so you must learn when to stop. To begin with the dog should be rewarded immediately when he comes into position, but as he grows more confident the titbit should sometimes be held back in your hand in order to teach the static stand without the dog becoming agitated. You may wish to use your key word for 'Leave' if the dog is particularly persistent, but don't introduce this restriction to soon, the dog must be happy to come into position before you build on time.

You can then show the dog the flat of your right hand, as he rises into the stand, your thumb and forefinger holding the titbit, and this will become your hand signal for the stand position.

Another favoured method for teaching the stand is to have the dog in the sit position, stand at the side facing the dog. Hold your lead in your left hand, sweep your right hand forward as a signal, and push your left foot under the dog's body, encouraging his hind legs backwards, and thus he must stand. This is not meant to startle or hurt the dog, and no pressure should be a burden upon the dog. The action should be more of a gentle teasing of the legs from the ground. Later you could use the leg signal to bring the dog into the stand, because if your training is correct he will comply as soon as he sees you shifting your weight onto your right foot. Be careful that the action does not appear too fast and so be misconstrued by the dog (or spectators) to be a kick. Once again introduce the key word once you have perfected the technique and you are sure of what you are doing. The word that you chose is not as important as its usage, I use different words for different types of stand. For DC I say 'Back', for a conformation stand I say 'Up', and for the stay I say 'Stand'. I use different words because I want slightly different things from each of the positions. The dog is capable of learning that there is a difference in what you require simply from your body posture and physical gestures even if you do use the same words. But when teaching a young dog many things and requiring so much precision, I like to try and make things as simple as possible for the dog and myself!

Building time and space.

Once you have correctly taught the dog the three positions you can then start to introduce a little time and distance. As usual we will go a little at a time building confidence all the time. Many occurrences of good controlled exercises will be far better than one long one that keeps going wrong. I can still hear my very first instructor yelling, if your dog breaks, you've gone too far too fast. How easy it is to ignore this advice, and to fall into the habit of continual correction. Remember that what the dog ends up doing is what he has learnt to be correct, irrespective of what you do to amend things afterwards. So it is imperative to get your basics have sound foundations and the dog has developed a confident attitude.

Be ready, as you move from the dog if he shows any signs of confusion or moving, you must help him to remain correct. Notice I don't say be ready to correct him, correction teaches nothing except that 'if you move you will be put back again', some dogs grow to enjoy this game, others become confused and anxious as their handlers grow more frustrated.

I start each session right by the dog even when he is, what I would class as, reasonably well trained. This way I am reminding him what it is that I want. Let us take the sit as an example, but the same procedure will apply to all three positions. Place the dog in the correct position, as his bottom comes to the floor give him the key word *'Sit'*. Once you are happy that he is relaxed and confident lean your body away from him, keeping your feet still to start with. As you begin to lean repeat your key word and be ready for any faltering on the dog's part. Lean back and reward and then release, remember your *timing, (see Concepts section if in doubt).* The next stage is to take a step away from the dog. Again set him up carefully, make sure that he is fully aware of what you are trying to do. Give him the key word *'Sit'* and adjust the lead to the back of his neck, hold it up and away from the dog to give you good control and then, when you are sure that the dog is stable, take a slow, smooth step away to the right with your right foot followed by your left foot. Encourage and give confidence with your voice and firmly but gently guide with the lead holding it above and behind his head. The tautness of the lead will give him confidence so long as you have not abused your lead usage in the past.

When you are sure that the dog is stable with you taking one step away from him you can build on to take another and then another and so on. The secret with the build up of this exercise is that the dog starts to learn that you mean the same thing even if the circumstances differ. So, this means taking the exercise from the beginning in differing places, at differing times, and with different people, animals or objects around. You must also sometimes be a little different yourself, perhaps change your coat or your perfume, all of these things can come into the equation of a dog's understanding of any number of situations. The first time that you change the situation with any relevance the dog may be very confused, be patient and treat it as a brand new exercise again, he will soon start to understand from your consistency that things are meant to be the same even when some of the variables differ. The section on understanding the dog's mind will help you to understand your dog's confusion. You must learn to think like a canine.

When your dog is confident in a given situation you can use this medium to build the exercise up and increase your time and space. Don't expect the dog to progress in leaps and bounds, take things a little at a time and get it right.

The next thing to do is to vary the length of time the dog is kept in position. I find counting to myself a great aid in self discipline. For instance I will set the dog up in the sit position, count to three, then return and release, then repeat counting to five return and release, then repeat counting to eight return and release, then repeat counting to two return and release. Of course you must be flexible, if the dog shows any signs of confusion or movement abandon your count and start again.

Avoid standing facing the dog, and watch that your hand position is not as it would be for the recall signal. It is easy for the dog to misconstrue your wishes reading your body stance. The dog watches body movement and gestures and interprets more from this than he does from verbal language.

When you have managed a couple of paces away from the dog in many different situations, and for varying lengths of time, it is appropriate to take things a stage further on. Each time you want to progress, remember to start from the beginning as if the dog knows nothing. This will build his confidence and help him to accept something new tagged onto the end of something he already knows. You could for instance decide that the dog is stable enough to take his lead off. To start this you must remain by his side, set him up as usual go through the routine for your normal procedure and then carefully unclip his lead. Keep the lead off for just a couple of seconds, then clip it back on to his collar. Reward and release. Do not release him from the exercise until his lead is re-connected to his collar, this will help to teach him not to move before the end of the exercise. The habit of re-connecting the lead will become part of the exercise and he is less likely to self release when it matters, i.e. in the ring!

It is useful to be able to train your dog with other dogs around and especially if you can work towards the sort of line up of dogs that you will experience in the ring. Don't forget to train your routine in this situation as all others, don't expect too much too soon, and certainly don't attempt to do things that you are not sure will work, even if everyone else around you appears to be more advanced. One of the biggest mistakes in dog training is trying to keep up with others. Everyone is different, everyone will have trained differently and for varying lengths of time. Your dog may be more immature, less confident, more easily confused. Don't make errors because of other people's pressure, remember that what the dog is **doing** is what he is **learning.** You can't afford to get it wrong too many times otherwise your dog training sessions will become perpetual re-training sessions and you will find it difficult to progress further. Remember you should go through the same dedication to the training procedure with all of the positions, don't assume that if the dog can do a two minute sit he will be able to do a two minute down without adequate training.

Preparing for the ring

Now that your dog can master the positions and is confidently working like a pro, introduce some of the sort of things that may go wrong in the ring. For instance what would your dog do if, as you left him you sneezed, had a coughing fit or dropped your dog lead? To be sure he will remain in position and that you are not going to blow your chances of winning the ticket just because pollen tickled your nose, train for it! Close on lead control to start with and then progressing to put in the distance. This means: standing by him to start with and then progressing to just as you leave him, and then at varying distances, pretend to cough, sneeze, drop something, chat to someone, basically introduce any of the things to your training that may happen to you in the ring, whether they are intentional or not.

What would your dog do if another dog started to wander around? You can teach your dog to ignore this by training with other dogs loose in the room or training area, make sure that they are friendly and pose no threat of course. Your own or dogs belonging to friends are good ones to start with.

What would your dog do if the patch of ground chosen for him to stay on has a particularly tempting smell? You can train to avoid the inevitable interest which may lead to a roll or change of position in order to get a better sniff. Put him in one of the positions   point to the floor and area around him and then use your key word *'Leave'*. *(See leave on command.)* Reward him for correct behaviour, but be ready to prevent him from getting things wrong by having him under control on lead.

What would your dog do if you left at an angle instead of straight? Train for it on lead. Give the key word, leave him in your chosen position, (start with his favourite), and then move across him, slowly and smoothly twist and turn, stand sideways,

Some of the summer campers with their dogs showing them that they don't have to see their handlers to enjoy the sit.

walk around him, turn every conceivable way, (not all at once of course), and all the time keep control with the lead, building the dog's confidence with your voice and positive handling, doing a little at a time.

What would your dog do if he became tired or bored with the position he was in? You can train for it. Have the dog on lead standing by your side, put him in position, let us say the *'sit'*.   Give him the key word *'sit '*, hold the lead in your right hand and apply gentle pressure with your left hand on his shoulders, as if you wanted him in the down but keep saying the key word *'sit'*. If the dog attempts to go down, and most will try at least to start with, lift him up with your lead in right hand and move your left hand to maintain the position of his rump as you

145

originally taught him. Repeat the key word *'sit'* and praise the dog when he is in the correct position. The dog will soon learn that in this situation, he must listen to the key words and ignore variables. As soon as he starts to actively resist the position change he must be rewarded so that he knows he is correct, but watch your timing, the reward must come as he resists in connection with your keyword, if you are a little late and he has relaxed he may take this further and misconstrue your reward as being for relaxing ready to change position. Work your way through any other position changes that may occur in the same manner, tempting the dog to alter position and then pleasantly reinforcing the key word position with confident, positive handling. There will of course be more than one possible change from each position and all of these should be covered. You will find that the most common changes are dropping from the sit to the down, and from the stand to the sit. It must be emphasised that you are not trying to fool the dog or catch him out, you are merely placing him in position, and making sure that he understands the meaning of the key word associated with that position. He will soon learn, and will enjoy pushing back against your hands in order to maintain the key word position. If your timing is correct, he will know that reward and your appreciation come for the correct action, and incorrect actions will be guided away until they become extinct.

Going out of sight

Going out of sight of the dog should never be rushed. When first attempted you should be out of your dog's sight for a very short time, seconds only. Leave the dog in his favourite position and in a very safe area where the dog feels confident.

To start with I like to turn my body sideways to the dog, and then progress to turning my back to him. You may well have already covered this in your ring craft training.

When you are very close to the dog you can feel any movement through the lead, but if you have done all of the above training correctly there should be no movement at all, if there is go back to your basics. A simple step in teaching the dog to accept you being out of sight as a starting exercise is to pass behind an obstacle or person and then immediately reappear. Your disappearance should be momentary only and if you then return to the dog and reward him in his position no problems should occur. It is only when you try to disappear for too long or in stressful situations that the problems will start to creep in. Make sure that once again the basics are covered well to avoid problems later. If the dog builds up oodles of confidence in training he will be able to cope with any minor disturbances or changes in the ring much more easily. Another good training experience can be done in the home or specially set up in the training hall using mirrors. If correctly positioned you can go out of sight around a corner or through a doorway but still see your dog and verbally give him help and encouragement when necessary. You can build in the silences that will occur when you are in the ring remotely, because you can see his reactions in the reflection on your mirror without him seeing you. You are then able to return to him if he looks unhappy and certainly before anything goes wrong. Of course to do this effectively you should not be physically very far away, you can't allow it to take very long to get back to him and you should only go on to this stage when you and the dog are ultra confident.

When training 'stays' for competition you should aim for a longer time than is required and then the dog will learn to be settled for suitable stretches of time. As often as possible you should train among other dogs, even if they are your own, but making efforts to get among other people's dogs as often as possible. If the only place that your dog meets other dogs is at a show, all is not lost, you can always get together with a few friends and enlist their help in a quiet corner of the show ground. But caution, be careful that the help you enlist doesn't interfere with your dog or show aggression even towards their own dog, as this is not going to have the required effect for your type of training. You must look for a good, sound, friendly atmosphere for teaching your dog.

Trouble shooting

Many handlers find stays a problem, and some of the keenest, stylish heel work dogs blow a good round with poor stays. When a handler comes to me with problems my advice is nearly always, as with most exercises, is to go right back to basics to the degree that you pretend that the dog knows nothing and retrain from the beginning. People find this difficult but it really is the best way. It builds confidence, and teaches the dog just what it is that you are trying to get at. The dog is not deliberately disobedient, he will purely react to a set of circumstances, sometimes circumstances have made the aims become distorted and when the dog becomes confused he uses his memory bank of triggered reactions to deal with things by himself. This is not always how we would like it. A sound basis to training will make things work for you.

*Summer Camper's dogs of levels from pre beginners to C all achieving a
confident Stand stay*

Sometimes there are faults that occur which only seem to arise in the ring. The
reason that this happens is normally that the basis of the training has not been
thorough enough. Occasionally something happens in the ring to frighten or
confuse the dog, a sudden thunderstorm, having to lie next to a dominant dog or be
disturbed by an aggressive handler even when it is not directed at your dog. In
cases like these we still go back to basics to give solid grounding for the dog, but
we may have to recreate the point at which the dog becomes confused and help
him through. For instance a friend's dog only broke within seconds of her leaving
with other handlers leaving at the same time. He had become spooked when
another dog did this in the ring once. So along with sound basics, we set this
situation up and helped the dog to overcome his confusion by on lead reward
based training amongst other handlers.

Sendaway

Before you start - The dog should be confident with you and you should have achieved 'the want'. The dog should also understand the basic static sit and down positions. You need to find a toy or titbit that he really likes, if using a toy it should of course be safe, and preferably not too big. An article that can be made smaller as time goes by is ideal, a piece of mat for instance, but this is not essential. It is more important that the dog loves his motivator. If using titbits you must obtain a pocket size tin that can be put down on the ground when you are training without the dog being able to help himself!

The sendaway should be great fun for both dog and handler. Fast, keen sendaways are achieved by creating a great desire for the dog to arrive at the given point. As with other exercises there are several methods of teaching, but the incentive methods are the most reliable.

All of the following procedures are done with the dog on lead and with you instigating great excitement. Try to be fast in your actions and create a good momentum.

Step one - Play with your dog and get him really motivated onto the article or titbit box.

Step two - Hold the dog's lead in your left hand, and your motivator in your right. Stand sideways on to the dog and show him the article, then move fanning backwards in a circular movement enticing the dog to run around, forward and towards the toy/tin. The object of the exercise is to get the dog looking in the direction that you are pointing. At this stage the dog will actually be going around in a circle, but this doesn't matter. The important factor is that he is enjoying going towards the toy. Let him move few steps at a time and then reward him with his toy or titbit. If you are using the tin of titbits it is a good idea to have some in the tin and some in your hand. You need to get to them quickly in order to keep up the momentum, the dog must think that they come from the tin in order for there to be sufficient motivation involved, but sometimes it is easier to cheat a bit. So long as the dog knows that treats come out of the tin, and that he gets one when the tin is in your hand then the method will work. Once you have the dog doing this introduce the key word that you want to use for the dog to look towards a

Sendaway

sendaway, I use the word *'Look'*. When you have completed this stage you have him looking in the direction that you are pointing on the key word *'Look'*.

Step three - Now we introduce the sendaway command. I use the key word, *'Go'*. Hold the dog back with his lead using your left hand. Stand forward of and sideways to the dog with your toy in your outstretched right hand. Excite the dog into looking at his toy, when he is looking give the key word *'Look'*, and then when the dog is raring to go introduce your keyword *'Go'* and let him run towards, and be rewarded with the article.

Step four - Now we must introduce a fast down. To get a good down in the ring the dog must understand that in order to get his reward he must go down immediately that he hears the key word. To ensure this the training is quite specific. We will progress as step two, but then as the dog is going around at a decent speed we introduce the down. To do this you bring the motivator to the floor in front of the dog. The action should be carried out with urgency and excitement. Try to keep the toy covered by your hand. Stop the dog in his tracks by halting your left hand and dropping it to the floor. Then swiftly move your left hand to the dog's back just at the base of his shoulders to help push him into the down. You may then have to run your hand down to his backside to push it over because some dogs halt in the play mode, i.e. bum in air. Follow this up by releasing the reward between the

The dog must go into the down before gaining the reward. Pat Leverick rewards Ross, her rescue dog, with his tug toy.

dog's two front feet whilst he stays in the down. Be careful to ensure that the reward is well within his reach, we do not want him to get into the habit of crawling forward or sniffing to find his reward, it must always be immediate. Many a ticket has been lost by allowing this very fault to creep in. At this stage of the training procedure it is quite easily avoided. Once you are confident of your handling of this stage, introduce the key word for dropping the dog. I use *'Down'*. Do not over do the instant down training for the first few sessions as you may find in your dog, a reluctance to 'Go' if he thinks that the only way to get his reward is to be in the down position. So combine all of the above steps at each session in order to keep up the momentum and avoid apprehension.

To give confidence and get the dog excited enlist the help of a friend or trainer to hold your dog and then run.....

Run to the sendaway area in a straight line, Sheila is positioned to get Flash into a down immediately and before he is rewarded with his ball

Step five - When you and the dog are confident in all of the above, and have trained in varying situations and environments you can introduce the next stage, which is to put in some distance. It is useful at this stage if you can get the dog to stay in a position when you leave him a few paces, although it is not imperative and if you are unsure of his stability tie him up or have a friend hold him, rather than have him ignoring your key words. The first stage is to place your motivator just a few feet away, and then follow steps three and four. Go with the dog still on lead of course, and make sure he goes into a fast down before he gets the reward. On lead it is easy to control this and the lead can be used to stop the dog just before he reaches his quest. If your initial training is thorough the dog will be very keen by this stage and your timing will be put to the test. Allow yourself more space than you would expect in order to get the dog down. You will be surprised how fast he will be to get to the toy. The timing of your keyword *'Down'* is crucial it must leave your mouth momentarily before the tension goes on the lead to stop the dog. By momentarily I mean less than a quarter of a second! If the dog shows any reluctance to go or starts to decrease his speed go back to the relevant training steps to ensure that your dog is confident.

Gradually you can increase the distance a step at a time. The further the distance the more the chance of things going wrong, so be very careful and sure that the dog is confident before progressing. Be sure that the dog is going into the down when you say the key word, and prior to getting the reward before you allow so much distance that you cannot control it.

Step six - If your dog is good and stable in the static sit, leave him in position, (if he is unstable have someone hold him), place your motivator article about 2 metres away, and then stand to the side facing the toy. Give the dog his *'Look'* word to get his attention on to the area followed by his *'Sendaway'* word, and encourage him towards the area, patting the floor or waving the toy to motivate him. You are then there, in position to make sure he goes into an instant down before he is rewarded. Thus he is now going to the designated area, on his own.

Step seven - Train your dog in an area that will make his motivator less easy to see, train from stage one, don't miss any stages, to avoid confusion and build up gradually. Keeping the motivation level high all the time. This is the vital stage in teaching the dog to always expect to be rewarded even if at first he cannot see his reward. If you have a green toy for instance train on grass, if you have a dark toy choose a dark surface, tarmac or concrete. If you have a toy that is hard to disguise try training on longer grass, but be careful that you do not always choose the same surface as the dog may start an association with surface to exercise. You may therefore have to introduce more than one motivator. *(See Play training)*

Step eight - Follow stage six but this time stand at the side between the article and the dog, keep just a couple of steps from the article to start with as you are going to follow up the dog to make sure he goes down before getting his reward. When you are sure of this you can progress back towards the dog step by step until eventually you can stand with the dog and send him. The progression must be gradual and the dog must be kept well motivated all of the time. Do not try to build all these steps in one lesson, a few feet per session is more reliable. Always go back to the beginning, i.e. step one, and work quickly yet purposefully through, at the start of each session. If the dog shows any signs of apprehension or confusion you are going to far to fast.

Step nine - We are now going to introduce differing articles and obstacles for the dog to either go to or ignore. At a show the scene may be very complicated and the dog should learn to go to, through, onto, or wherever he is told. Start by introducing markers or obstacles scattered ad lib around your training area, train from stage one to avoid any confusion. Train for the dog to ignore completely to start with, your initial training will have taught him to look only for his toy.

An easy marker to teach the dog to recognise as a starting point is a mat. Set him up as you would for stage six, but with the toy placed to the back of the mat. You will be using his key words, *'Look'* and *'Go'* and now introducing the new key word *'Mat'*. Position yourself to ensure that your are able to drop the dog on the mat, and then follow up with his reward. Tell him *'Look - Mat'* and then an excited *'Go'*. Race with him to the mat, help him into the down, and reward. Whilst he is still on the mat point, at it, and say, *'Look - Mat, Good boy Mat'*. The emphasis being on the key words, any 'good boys' or 'brilliants' should be less obvious to the dog and the key words should come out very clearly. Remember what you are trying to achieve, this is not the meaning of *'Good boy'*, but the meaning of the new key words. Once again build this up as if it were a new exercise, because to the dog it is quite different, it may take a while for the new word to register a meaning.

Once he has mastered the above try another piece of common ring furniture like a pole. Exactly the same procedure, the toy placed just behind the pole set him up, say *'Look -Pole'*, and then *'Go'*, and follow it through. *'Cone'*, sending to one cone, and *'Box'*, sending to the centre of a box are two more useful associations for the competitive obedience ring.

Step ten - The dog can be taught to go into a box and ignore others. This will help him in ignoring other obstacles and ring furniture. Set up a box of cones or other articles in a large enough square for the dog to comfortably turn and drop at speed without knocking any. Place his toy on the back line of the box and then call him into the area. Make sure you are in full control, don't allow mistakes. Once he has successfully done this walk around to the opposite side, put him in the sit, show him the centre of the box and call him to it. When he has confidently done this a couple of times walk around to one side, repeat, and then the other side. To build the distance do it very gradually following all of the steps.

A similar procedure can then be followed setting up markers in four corners of a ring, sending the dog alternately to each of the areas. All this good positive training will help the dog to deal with ring situations. If you are not thorough like this, he will, when confronted with distractions, try to come to his own conclusions, normally homing in on the first thing he sees.

The dog is capable of learning many different associations. In order to avoid confusion think clearly about what you are trying to achieve, bob down to dog's eye level before making any assumptions. Don't just look at your objective, look beyond and consider all of the possibilities of the dog's eye view.

How does it work in the ring?

In training I never get to the stage where the motivator is taken away completely, but as the dog progresses and becomes ultra confident, then the article is placed so that it is not so easy to see, in fact sometimes it is hidden altogether, under a cone perhaps or behind a log. When it is hidden I run out to the dog and reveal it, or sometimes throw another toy to the dog from a short distance away. If you stick to the rule that the dog is always rewarded somehow, then the very few times that this is impossible, i.e. in the ring, the dog does not realise that it has happened, and in any case he is so keen to do the exercise by this time that it wouldn't matter anyway.

When you are competing at a show give yourself and your dog every opportunity of getting it right. Check out the ring and the send away that you will have to do. If it is at all possible train your dog at the show to something as similar as possible, in a similar sort of area. Don't forget that the sendaway set up in the car park may look totally different when set up out on the field. Look at the whole aspect of the area, any markers or ring poles used, the background, and beyond. Then, having gone to all of this trouble   **TRAIN - DON'T PRACTICE.**

Troubleshooting

With a very toy mad dog sometimes it is necessary to hide the toy most of the time just as the food for a titbit dog is concealed in a tin.

Occasionally I have found it necessary to use a toy for the motivation to go out to an area, calling the dog to it, and then as the progression takes place the toy is thrown out to or beyond the dog when he reaches the correct position, and is down. This method is only for dogs who are so hooked on toys that they cannot concentrate on anything else, and it is better to proceed to the stage where you choose a less motivating motivator if this is possible! You must be very careful using this technique that the dog does not try to come forward or hover waiting for the toy to be thrown. If he should do this, withdraw the reward, put it in your pocket and start the exercise again.

If a dog is unsure and has a tendency to drop short, do not chastise him as this will make his apprehension worse. It is better and more productive to reward the dog for the part that he gets correct. For instance having sent the dog he starts to hesitate. The second you identify this call out your key word for down, and run out and reward him for getting that far. Then start him off from there, show him where you want him, call him to the spot and reward him again. Set up the exercise again, this time starting the dog just a few feet before the position that he first dropped, put his motivator in the correct position, and send him. He will get nearer even if he does not get it right. The abundance of praise and reward comes of course when the dog is correct, but you should at first reward quite lavishly even when you have had to drop the dog incorrectly. This reward gives him confidence to go on, and you can adjust the level of reward to be a little less each time as he gets progressively nearer to the correct place, and the abundance of reward is then transferred to the correct place. So the attitude is something like this, the first time he goes wrong you are saying,
'Hey that was really good to get that far, I'm so pleased - now try this, hey that's even better!'. Next you are saying, 'Yes that's OK, but wow what a great dog I like that even better', and so on. Repeat as above until he gets the idea and then build your distance again. Don't be afraid to drop him early again if he shows any confusion or apprehension, and reward for what he did.

This method of training is called shaping, getting the dog nearer and nearer to what you are trying to achieve, and is the method used in dolphinariums to teach the dolphins to perform incredible feats on the blow of a whistle.

Sometimes dogs get what handlers call a block, they may have been doing sendaways for years and suddenly they can't get it right any more. This may have been caused by external interference, a stray dog in a ring, an aggressive judge, a freak storm, there are many possibilities. If this happens you must simply retrain, and set up situations similar to those that frighten the dog and train through them using high motivation techniques. You may simply have to do a lot of playing in certain situations, you may have to enlist the help of people who can act as judge or steward etc. Suffice to say that the problem won't just go away, you will need to set it up and train through it.

Sometimes the block is less easy to identify, but if you think it through, look at the point at which the dog starts to go wrong, and identify what is happening momentarily before that. In most cases, if the dog performs correctly in training then the linking or set up of the exercise is not the same in training as it is in the ring. You need an exact ring mock up, judges, stewards, ropes, furniture, procedure, warm up outside the ring, exercise linking the lot and then **train** through. *(See Linking).*

The Recall

The recall from the box is not really anything to do with teaching the sendaway, and certainly should only very rarely if ever be linked together with the sendaway in training, if you wish to avoid anticipation or fidgeting in the sendaway area. The training of the recall to the heel position is covered in the recall section. It is necessary to build up a little time that the dog is held in the down position, prior to a recall command, and so when the dog is doing very good confident sendaways you can introduce some walking around before going back to reward him, keeping your eye on him and remind him

Yvonne demonstrates with Holly the perfect Sendaway, the dog going into the position, and watching alert, for the next request from Yvonne

'Down' whilst you walk around. It is also useful to throw in the odd 'Call your dog' as the steward would say in the ring to accustom the dog to hearing this phrase, but learning to ignore it. If you don't work against things like this they can become stimulus to the dog to perform the next act, and therefore in ring terms we have anticipation. The dog is not being naughty, but merely acting on learnt stimulus, really he is just being a dog. With the very keen, actively competing dog the words 'Call your dog' should be followed by your 'Down' word, to ensure the dog realises that he must listen to your words only.

Distance Control   (DC)

Before you start the dog should enjoy and be well motivated by his toy or a titbit. He should have acquired 'The Want'. You should decide on what words you will use, the tones of voice those words will be spoken, and you should practice saying the words and throwing your voice over a distance. When you train the dog the same tones should be used at close quarters.

What is Distance Control ?
(or DC as it tends to be abbreviated to)

The ultimate goal of the exercise is to leave the dog in a position, (sit, down or stand), as indicated by the judge, go a minimum of 10 paces (more, at the discretion of the judge), and then on the instructions of the judge or steward, tell the dog to change position six times in sequence. Each judge that you work under will decide on what the sequence will be that day. The dog should not move more than a body length in any direction. This always seems a little unfair on the small breeds, but then their stride is arguably shorter, so *quid pro quo*. Each change of position should be clean and smart. The handler is then instructed to return to the dog's side. For each change of position the handler is allowed only one command or signal, together with the dog's name. Some handlers opt to use variations in the tonation of the dog's name, either with the command or signal, or on its own.

For a beginner the exercise sounds complicated, but if you start early you will enjoy teaching this fun exercise. By the time you need it in the 'C' class you will feel confident and so will the dog. Even if you don't see yourself hitting these dizzy heights DC is always an impressive party piece.

All of the DC positions can be taught by physically manipulating the dog, or by using a toy or titbit to motivate and direct the dog into position. The latter is more fun and is in most cases much easier for both dog and handler. A ball is the easiest motivator to use, because you can throw the ball for the dog to catch and it will be an instant reward when he goes into the correct position. A squeaky ball is even better because it works twofold, obviously it can be thrown but also, the squeak can be used to maintain attention when necessary. Other toys will work equally well so long as the dog is sufficiently motivated by them. Make sure that your toy

Distance Control

your toy is safe. *(See Toys and play training before you start).* Be very careful with your body posture, signals and even your intake of breath, the dog will learn to read your every move. Teach him to move when you give a clear keyword or signal and not before. It looks really cute when the dog takes up position as soon as you take a preparatory breath ready to say the next position, but it is difficult for the judge to decide whether the dog has anticipated or not. Leave no room for doubt, because doubt means points lost.

Step one - Start on lead, although you will soon find that you can dispense with the lead as the dog starts to enjoy this exercise. Hold your lead in your left hand and your toy in your right. Excite the dog with your 'Switch on' words, *('Ready, steady'),* and with the toy, get him playing. Keep your lead fairly short. When you are confident that the dog is happy, manipulate him so that he is playing in front of you. Step forward into the dog. At the same time raise your right hand and toy up above his head aiming backwards to bring him into a natural sit. Your left hand will come up and help the dog into a sit position. You may have to adjust your hand and lead positioning until you get this right. The dog should automatically and happily go back into the sit position. The movement that must be achieved is a backward movement. The dog's front feet should sweep back to meet his back feet. He may even jump back into the sit if he is the excitable type, this is fine. Immediately he is in position say *'Sit'*, and throw the ball into his mouth for him to catch. As he catches say *'Catch'*. If he misses, go with him and encourage him to get the toy, say *'Get it'*. Don't let him clear off to get it on his own,

Smudges' favourite exercise, the ball is his motivator but he will do this now for the sheer fun of it!

Distance Control

remember 'team work'. As soon as he has the toy put your right hand into his mouth and take or prise the toy out, by doing this you are entering into the game and the dog doesn't feel threatened, you are not giving commands to release, you are creating team spirit, and avoiding a stand off situation.   If the dog holds on too hard, is very keen, or has a particularly hard grip then you can use your key word *'Leave'*, but remember to keep it light and fun. Repeat this a couple of times at each training session or whenever you have the opportunity at home, until it starts to become automatic. Play, play, play. Step towards him. Raise your right hand above him. Say *'Sit'* as he comes into position. Throw the ball say *'Catch'* as he catches it. Take the ball from his mouth and carry on playing. Try to keep up the momentum. Make your actions swift, clear and fun.

Step two - Now we will introduce the stand position. Sometimes it is easier to put the dog in the sit as above first and then to bring him into the stand. The basic procedure is similar, so experiment and see which you find the easiest.   You should choose the easiest, because once the dog can do this the other manoeuvres will be much more easy for him to understand. This step deals with getting the stand straight from play, step three tells you how to do it from a sit, use which ever you find easiest. The suggested key word to use for stand is *'Back'*. The reason is that most people find it easier to say with any volume, and so the dog will be able to hear at the distance required in the ring, also it cannot be anticipated on the *'S'* part of the word and misconstrued as *'Sit'.*

Get the dog in *'play mode'* with his toy. Manipulate the play until he is in front of you. Have your lead in your left hand and your toy in your right. Position your toy at dog nose height. Take a step or

Yvonne Hollyoak's Jimmy shows sheer enjoyment on his face learning to do the DC STAND position

159

two towards the dog so that he steps back away from you. Push the toy forward, still at nose height, hold the toy still, as the dog becomes stationary say *'Back'*. Throw him the toy, say *'Catch'*. Play. Take the toy from the dog and repeat several times. The dog may take several steps back before becoming stationary, this doesn't matter in fact it has positive benefits. It means that he is taking a active measure towards backward movement. In the ring tendencies are for the dog to come forward towards the handler at each change in position, because the dog is isolated and wants to be with the handler. If the dog is trained to go back into each position this tends to compensate. As part of your training you can extend this movement, and keep walking toward the dog so that he walks backwards. Repeat your key word *'Back'*. Take this a few steps at a time and always reward and play as part of the exercise.

Step three - Teaching the stand from the sit. Play the dog into the sit position as step one. Next, with excitable dogs simply step forwards into the dog. Push the toy forwards in line with the dog's nose, and make the action appear as though you are going to go right through the dog. Normally the dog will spring back up into the stand position. As soon as the dog is in the stand tell him *'Back'* and reward him. With some dogs you may need to place your left foot in between the front and hind legs to gently push the dog's hind legs back into the stand position to start. This should not be a kick but merely a gentle prise to manipulate the dog's back legs back into the stand. As soon as the dog is in position say *'Back'*, and reward him with his toy. Soon he will start to come up into the stand as soon as your leg starts to move. Repeat at each training session until the dog becomes confident.

Step four - Teaching the down from the stand. This is an easy move, play the dog into the stand position. Hold your lead in your left hand and your toy in your right. When the dog is settled in the stand bring your toy swiftly down between his two front paws, and at the same time pull back and down with your lead to hinge the dog back into the down position. As soon as he is down say the key word *'Down'*, and release his toy. He may flop his body over as if doing a down for stays, it is best to ignore this. If you start handling him too much he may become apprehensive and feel pressured. We can alter this body position and get him into the correct sphinx style down by using the reward and sit position in the next step. Repeat until the dog is happy going down whatever his position as long as he does not come forward into it, and then go onto the next step.

Step five - Teaching the sit from the down. The dog has already learnt the signal for the sit position in step one. To get him from the down to the sit is a very similar procedure. Use your toy in your right hand to lift up and over his head sweeping him back and up into the sit. Use your lead to help him in the right direction, and you may find it useful, particularly with the heavier dogs to push back with the inside of your right foot across the dog's front feet. The aim is for his front feet go back to meet his back feet, and not visa versa. Some dogs get very excited when training and the fault that may creep in here is that the dog lifts his bottom and has a tendency to stand before sitting. This is not acceptable so make sure that you control it with your lead to avoid the problem.

Step six - The sit from the down once perfected will aid to teach the dog to do the sphinx down. Once the dog is confident doing the down in any style he likes, withhold the reward following the down, and bring him immediately into the sit using the upward sit signal with hand and toy, and then reward. Repeat this several times and the dog will start to work out for himself that it is easier to come into the sit and gain the reward from the sphinx than it is from the rolled over or flat down position.

Step seven - Teaching the down from the sit. Play the dog into the sit, when he is confident and attentive, bring the toy down between his two front feet as in stage four. Again the main problem will be if the dog lifts into the stand first so to avoid this, have your left hand ready to aid him into the down by pushing back and down on his shoulders. Watch the positioning of your hands, the dog will tend to follow them so make sure they are low and giving a backwards movement.

Jan Davies Diva is just learning the perfect sphinx DOWN position, the toy is aimed between the front paws to prevent forward movement.

Step eight - Teaching the stand from the down. This is probably the most difficult to perfect, as there is no straight forward natural movement that will easily show the dog what is wanted, it must therefore be a combination of moves. It is

161

important to avoid forward movement in all position changes, but this is the combination that will bring the dog forward if anything does. To avoid forward movement it is necessary to over exaggerate the backward movement in training. Play the dog into the down, have your toy in your right hand, lead in your left, when the dog is keen but settled, walk forwards into him, holding your right hand at nose height, bring your lead low and back over the dog's back, and be ready if necessary to sweep his back legs back with your left foot. This should all flow together, and should be approached with a pleasant, well motivated attitude as usual. Once the dog is in the stand continue to walk him a few steps backwards with your toy still at nose height. Repeat a few times at each session and the dog will soon be trotting backwards quite enthusiastically. If the dog tends to go sideways work against a wall or other barrier to help him to learn to go straight.

Step nine - Now we have covered all the combinations, and the dog is confident and enthusiastically going into them, it is time to introduce a few link ups. This is done with exactly the same attitude as before, making it all fun, and following the procedures as above. Do not be tempted to run more than one extra move at a time. If you link too soon the dog may lose confidence. The combination to start with could be, sit-stand-sit, for instance. This is relatively easy and a good place to start. When the dog has perfected this, try sit-stand-sit, then down-sit-down, then stand-sit-stand, and so on. Always aiming to make it easy for the dog. Choose the combinations of positions that the dog and you find enjoyable first. Don't fall into the trap of getting carried away sequencing, throw in some positions on their own and reward them. If the dog does a position and it is not 100% correct go back and put in every aid to get it right, and don't forget to reward the dog. If the dog shows any apprehension or anticipation use your reward to get the dog into the correct mode, i.e. if he starts springing into the stand before you tell him, put in a sit with immediate reward.

Step ten - When the dog has perfected these combinations, then you can try combinations with three different moves. Stand-sit-down, and so on. Don't forget to keep on throwing easy ones in, like a simple sit on its own to give the dog confidence.

Step eleven - Now the dog is able to do all of the above it is time to teach him about distance. This should be done very gradually, starting from the beginning, one position at a time. He must learn that it is OK to do it at a distance. He will not understand what is wanted unless you apply the distance teaching principle to all positions and combinations. Building up distance is very simple, but you must be patient and refrain from racing on too fast. Start with your dog's favourite position. Put him into it, give him his key word take a couple of steps away from him, repeating the keyword, throw him his reward, *'Catch'*. Try this on all three single positions, talk the dog through giving confidence. The dog will probably have no problem, but check to make sure, and retrain if necessary.

Step twelve - This time decide on the dog's favourite combination. Leave him in a position and from just a couple of paces away give him his keyword for the change of position. Use your body posture as in the initial training making as if going towards him and following it through to help him if necessary. As he goes into position throw his ball to reward him, *'Catch'*. This can then be progressed to all of the combinations.

Step thirteen - When the dog is confidently doing the combinations with you a couple of paces away, you can start to gradually reduce the amount of extra body movement and signals that you give. Make smaller movements, and stop as soon as the dog is in position, but follow up with immediate reward. Sometimes your reward can be the toy at other times just show the toy and reward with your voice. The toy can start to go in and out of sight, and be used when it is needed to give confidence. *(See eliminating aids)*.

Step fourteen - At this point we have not taught the dog that we will be starting the exercise from the heel position. If we don't spend a little time on this, it will come as a shock when we need to set the dog up in the ring. The dog by now should be very confident, practice playing him into position at your side. Play with him on lead get him motivated, and then manoeuvre through your play until he is by your side. Use your hand signal with your toy, aid him manually with your lead, hand or foot if necessary, into the position. Choose his favourite position first, place him and reward. Keep it light and fun. Introduce a key word for DC that tells the dog that although he is wanted in the heel position he is not about to do heel work. Most people use the word *'Control'*. So the procedure will follow on like this: play with the dog, manoeuvre him into position, then say *'Control - Sit'*, and use your hand signal and lead to position him by your side, release and play. The dog may not be in a perfect position to start with but this will gradually come if you encourage and reward at the correct time.

Step fifteen - Now the dog is at the stage where he can be left from the heel position, and you can work a couple of paces away and with a minimal amount of help, it is time to start very gradually increasing the distance. This **must** be done gradually and the exercise should be split, repeatedly returning to the dog to reward him, and/or throwing the toy from the distance. This should be progressed

Distance Control

building up a pace at a time, for each position and combination of positions. Start with a single position leave the dog a couple of metres and then return, next leave a couple of metres and give a change of position being ready to help with all of your signals and walk back towards the dog if necessary, the signals from your body and voice should be sufficient for the dog to understand if your basics have been thorough. After each position or combination return to the dog talking in a soothing way, quietly helping him to stay put. If he moves stand still and talk to him, when he is still reward him immediately from the distance. Think about what you are trying to achieve if the dog starts to do something wrong, just stop put it right and reward it immediately.

Don't, just because the dog reaches a certain standard in this exercise, continually go through the finished article. The dog must be given confidence, and the precision will be kept up by continuing to break the exercise down to the basic level in training.

Scent Discrimination

Dogs have around 220 million scent receptors in their noses. Balanced against our mere 5 million this is pretty impressive. The dog can identify scents which are so diluted that we do not have instruments to measure them. The odours that the dog comes into contact with have an effect on his behaviour, indeed odours have an extremely powerful influence on the dog's life.

When a dog sniffs and takes a scent he takes the odour over a bony structure called the subethmoidal shelf (humans don't have one of these), and onto the lining of the nasal membranes. When the dog breathes normally the scent molecules remain in nasal chambers and accumulate in nasal mucus, the chemical odour then sticks to receptor cells. These receptor cells convert the chemical odour into electrical signals that send messages to the various parts of the brain responsible for dealing with the particular message or emotion.

The dog is much more of an expert than we at the art of taking scent, and although we can influence some of the odours that he takes, if he experiences a bad association we must be very patient and sympathetic in our training, and learn to work with the dog's natural abilities rather than trying to force them.

Teaching scent is an exciting experience for both dog and handler. The basis of scent can be taught in the early days whilst the puppy is still restricted to safe areas like the house and garden due to inoculation incubation. You can be kept busy and your dog will be learning to learn in the process.

Avoid wearing perfumes or scented hand creams, these are very strong with false smells, and will not help the dog to learn the exercise that we need him to achieve.

If you are just starting scent training with an adult dog, don't be afraid to treat him like a pup and follow these first stages of training. Even adult dogs need to learn how we want them to discriminate, and the procedure that we would like them to follow.

Early scent training should be done on a familiar article, knotted sock or toy, and later progressed to a variety of familiar articles that the dog can enjoy relating to and will want to find. The use of a fabric article for training is a good idea as all scent discrimination in Kennel Club obedience competition in the UK is done on cloth at the time of this book going to press. Having said that it is advisable to have a few differing textures and materials, and include a variety of substances e.g.

plastic, nylon, card, wood and even metal in your training bag to add interest and awareness as the dog progresses.

There is nothing more natural for very young pups than to follow scent trails, they are genetically programmed to do so from the nest onwards. This is a defence mechanism to prevent them from straying too far from the nest. This develops as a hunting and social skill later on. It is a simple task for we humans to elaborate on this superb doggy skill, but yet a task that often goes badly wrong because we try to apply human emotions and characteristics to canine behaviour. In essence we must try to think like a dog.

One of the major stumbling blocks in teaching scent discrimination is the struck dumb approach! Many handlers perfect the early stages but then once any formal training starts to take place they seem unable to move from the spot or speak! Scent is like any other exercise and the dog needs to learn what we want from him. Yes, he has a more superior nose than us, but this does not mean that he automatically knows what we want him to do with it! He can probably run faster and better than us too, but we still continue to teach him and perfect how we want fast pace to be developed, even after he has started to use it in the ring. So don't be afraid of communicating with the dog, be with him, help him, show him what you want. Don't leave him hovering over a scent pattern getting more and more confused.

Step one - Choose a favourite toy or rag, bring yourself to dog level, sit on the floor with a smaller dog or puppy, a low non restrictive chair may be useful with a larger dog, and play. Have the dog on a lead so that you can reel him in to you, and have a food or toy treat to encourage him just as in the first stage of retrieve. When he takes the article if he knows them use your key words *'Hold'* and *'Come'*. Help him all the way to make sure he comes back, with the article, produce your food as he comes towards you, but try to avoid him dropping the article to take the food. If he does not yet understand *'Hold'* and *'Come'* this is covered in the retrieve section. You can still do these first few stages even without, simply by taking the article from the dog's mouth. If your basic *'Want'* training is good the dog will be happy to come back to you for a cuddle and the continuance of the hide and seek game will be motivation enough i.e. he is rewarded by you for not stopping the game. If you can manage without the food lure at this stage, you will find that the pup is less distracted, but if you need to use it do so.

Step two - Teach your dog to take scent from your hand or from an article. We will start with your hand. Food is always a good incentive so, to start with, handle some smelly titbits like liver. Let the dog approach your hand hold the titbit in your fingers and let him take it. Next take a titbit, and hold it between your finger

Scent Discrimination

and palm, hold out your forefinger and thumb as if the titbit were there and let the dog sniff , as he does this introduce the new key word *'Smell'*. Once he is doing this, transfer the titbit to the other hand for rewarding. Still use your right hand offered to the dog in the same gesture for him to take scent, but as soon as he smells your hand bring out the reward from the other hand. Increase the time that he is sniffing slightly, and then reward. Next introduce a toy or rag that you will be using for scent and repeat the procedure using the food or his favourite toy as reward when he sniffs. Next let him sniff his favourite toy and reward him with it. Soon he will be sniffing anything you ask him to.

Step three - Once you have the dog interested and stimulated, allow him to watch you put the scent toy under your hand and then encourage him to try to get it. As soon as he acknowledges that he knows where the article is, reward him with it. Repeat the exercise, over several sessions until the dog becomes confident.

Step four - Once the dog is confidently acknowledging, and actively seeking out the article, introduce your key word for go and search, I use the word *'Find'*. Let him sniff the article, try to hold your hand open in a posture that will be used later when he takes scent without an article there. Hold him back for a few seconds whilst he watches you put the article out of sight somewhere in close proximity, under your leg for instance, and then release him on the key word *'Find'*. Encourage him to seek out the article, help him if necessary by indicating in the general direction of the hiding place. Call him so that he knows to come to you when he has the article. Reward him as above and repeat the exercise. Once he is keen and finding the article easily, restrict the prize for a few moments. This is easily done by holding down your leg, for seconds only, just long enough for him to really use his nose and acknowledge the scent.

Step five - When you are happy that the dog is stimulated to find on the key word and is very confident, change the hiding place to perhaps under your other leg, behind your back etc., still let him see where the toy went. The more confident he gets the more hiding places you can try, but remember make it easy, train for success. You will enjoy progressing this to hiding the toy behind furniture, under a rug, etc. Keep introducing the *'Smell'* word as well and encouraging the dog to take the scent of what he is going for before he goes, sometimes directly from the article, sometimes from your hand.

Step six - Now we have the dog taking scent, searching and finding his article, so at this point it is a good time to try a different article, thus he learns to enjoy the exercise with a different motivation. You should choose a familiar and fun article

167

Scent Discrimination

and the dog should enjoy holding it. Start at step one again. It is very tempting to start where you left off with the first article, but this is a dangerous thing to do. The dog has to learn that you mean the same thing again, and to be sure that he knows, give him all the help you can by starting from the beginning. It won't take very long, and the more times you are successful, the more chance you have of succeeding in the long run. When he is happy with this try an article belonging to someone else, so that the introduction of a foreign smell is not alien to him, and he will happily adjust if, to start with at least, the article is fun.

Step seven - Apply all of the above training stages in varying environments and terrains, i.e. halls, fields, gardens friends houses, etc. also with differing textures, and other people's articles. With each new environment or article, start at stage one. Have the dog on lead so that you can guide and control his actions.

Step eight - Take your dog into an area of long grass and play with him and his toy. Drop the article into the grass and let him retrieve it. Hold him back by his collar and throw the toy a meter or so away, when he is raring to go release the hold on his collar and let him find the toy. Of course it is best to still have hold of the end of the lead to avoid any problems of the dog wandering of and being distracted, it is unlikely that this would happen if the dog is sufficiently motivated, but it is better to be safe than sorry. If for any reason he doesn't acknowledge the article, he should start searching straight away, call him back and go down to ground level with him as per steps one, two, three etc. until he gets the hang of it. Repeat this stage several times making sure that the dog becomes confident. Sometimes letting him take scent from your hand sometimes from the article. Taking scent is now becoming part of the game.

Step nine - Walk with your dog in the grass do heel work if you wish or just play, drop the article behind you as you go, take the dog to within just a few feet of where you dropped it, turn him towards where it has fallen, point to it and send him using his key word to *'find'*. Keep your voice exciting and motivational. Remember this is supposed to be fun so enjoy it. Don't leave the dog on his own if he looks apprehensive or stops working, go out to him get involved and help. Call the dog to you when he has the article and make a great fuss of him. We are teaching scent so it is not necessary to put in a present and finish, simply call and praise him. Take the article from him and repeat or go on to something else.

At this stage you can start to introduce some off lead work, try just dropping the lead to start with, and then if you are sure that the dog is not distracted by anything else you can try some short off lead search backs. If you do not find that the dog is ready for this don't worry you can proceed on lead all the way through

Scent Discrimination

the training. In each section you will be doing some on and some off lead, building confidence in freedom, but making sure that accuracy and concentration is not sacrificed for freedom. In other words make sure that every stage is good on lead before releasing the dog to do it lead free. Just because the dog is released this doesn't mean you should let him work on his own, still help him go out into the scent area with him and generally make sure that all goes according to plan.

Step ten - Follow step nine and increase the distance of search back, change the article, and generally vary the area that you drop the article. Don't do all this at once. Choose one of the above, let us say that you decide on this occasion to change the article. Just do a short search and make it really easy for the dog to start with. Once the dog is confident on his article gradually increase the distance of search by half a meter at a time. Do **not** train on one item for too long, it is better to do a short session and then change to something else, and then come back and pick up a step or two back from where you left off.

Step eleven - Find in the environment, out on a walk or in the garden some obstacles, stones, boulders, hay bales, etc. and hide your article behind these and have fun with your dog sending him to find it. This valuable step need never be forgotten and any time that you are out walking your dog, whether he works the beginner class or the ticket class you can enjoy this game in the knowledge that it is giving your dog confidence for scent.

Caution - try to avoid sending the dog over areas where the article has been dropped previously. The reason for this is that the dog will be able to smell the scent still lingering on the ground, from where the article lay before and he may become confused. The more experienced he becomes the more confused he will be if you make this error, because he becomes accustomed to picking up the scent rather than a specific article. We could through training teach him to ignore the scent unless the article is obviously there but then this will result in the dog not attempting to pick up a less obvious articles. Cloth the same colour as the ground or laid very flat on concrete, will tend to be ignored by dogs taught to ignore lingering scents left by articles. So it is better to avoid the problem than to create one.

So far so good, you have taught the dog to find a variety of known and unknown articles in a variation of environments, ignoring other obstacles, and scents. Now to bring things out in the open a little more, and to start to simulate ring conditions.   Introducing formality is where things normally start to go wrong because handlers want to go too far too fast. It is possible to teach an adult dog

Scent Discrimination

*to perform a good basic scent discrimination fairly quickly **if** you don't miss out any stages. With the older dog that already understands some basic key words like sit, hold, come etc., and is easily motivated, the exercise can be ring worthy within a week, but no stages should be missed to ensure that the dog is confident and enthusiastic, and this will create a lasting ability to discriminate accurately.*

Step twelve - Select some objects to use as neutral articles, i.e. articles that are not to be selected by the dog as correct. These should be things that are not easy or attractive for the dog to pick up, we do *not* want him to touch them. Wall or floor tiles, preferably light colour, are ideal because they are square like a cloth. If you are handy at woodwork, or know someone who is, you can make, (or have made) some scent boards. These are wooden boards the size of a scent cloth, and on to them you pin scent cloths. This is an ideal training aid, it looks like the real thing but it is not easy for the dog to pick them up. To make this even more authentic you need one board without a cloth, and this one will be used to place your own scent on. If you use this system you should keep *your* board for *your* scent separate from the others. It doesn't matter if you handle *your* board but you must not handle the neutral articles or boards. If you do handle them, you must protect them from *your* scent by using thick, dense, rubber gloves or better still metal tongs. If you use tongs don't be fooled into thinking that metal doesn't carry scent, because it most certainly does. Don't touch the end of the tongs that you are going to handle the articles with, and don't handle with them, any items that *you* have handled previously, as this will transfer your scent. If you can imagine putting your fingers into a pot of paint, and then handling various items, you finger prints would show up on everything that you touch and the traces of paint would be passed onto any article that came into contact with those that you had touched, not only that the fumes from the paint can linger on items that have not even been touched, but have been in the vicinity. Scent transfers in a similar way except that unfortunately we can't see it, so we must be ultra careful in what we handle so as not to inadvertently confuse the dog and spoil all of our hard work.

To give you an example of how scent can transfer; a drug detector dog in Florida identified a drugs haul by finding the scent of cocaine on money that had at some time, been hidden behind the dashboard of a car but was no longer there when the police brought the car and driver in on another offence. Such was the trust in the dog's ability that although nothing was found behind the dashboard when the dog identified that something was there, the prisoner was interrogated and eventually the truth came out.. The money had been handled by drug dealers, and hidden there the previous week. My own drug detector dog can find the scent of where something was hidden inside a refrigerator, months ago.

When you have selected the necessary training paraphernalia you are ready to start the next stage.

Introducing the formal exercise

Step thirteen - Place one neutral article or scent board on the ground, and let the dog see you throw his favourite scent article out. Go out with the dog and encourage him to pick up the correct article using the appropriate key words. We are not asking for formalisms at this stage, only success. So make sure you are with the dog helping all of the way, allow him to sniff the neutral article if he wants, if he lingers too long, encourage him to identify and pick up his own article. Once he has satisfied himself that the other articles are boring and not suitable for picking up, he will learn to ignore them just as he did the boulders etc. when he first began his scent training. This is a very important lesson for the future. To learn to check and ignore incorrect articles. It is not imperative that the dog checks every article, some dogs always take scent on the air and don't seem to need to get their nose down. I do think it makes sense to not get too strung up over this and to leave the actual physical technique of scenting to the expert with the 220 million scent receptors!

Step fourteen - Place on the ground two neutral articles or boards. Once again throw the dog's article in amongst or beyond them. Send him out as above, aiding him in every way to guarantee success.

Step fifteen - When he is confidently bringing in the article in step fourteen, try walking with him past the neutrals, dropping the article, and sending him back as in stages eight and then nine.

Step sixteen - It is still best to use your scent boards. Place your own board, i.e. the plain board that you will use for *your own* scent, in-between the other two, each approximately a meter apart. Choose one of your dog's knotted cloth articles and place it on the centre board. Distract him from the situation for a few moments with a little game, and then set him up very close to the boards. Point to the area, let him sniff your hand, and then send him out, go with him to give him confidence.

Step seventeen - When the dog is confident in step sixteen, untie the cloth, and try the exercise again, it will look slightly different to the dog so he may be a little apprehensive to start with, so help him do a play retrieve in the opposite direction on the open cloth, aim for success.

Step eighteen - Add another board to the neutrals, and repeat as steps sixteen and seventeen. You can now start to build up to a maximum of ten boards. Don't do this all in one session, and at each new training session start with the basic search back and fun scent training before going on to this more formal side.

Introducing Patterns

Step nineteen - The boards need not necessarily be laid in a straight line, some times just put them out ad-lib, sometimes put out a pattern, a 'T' shape for instance or a circle. Sometimes standing away from the articles a little, other times standing in the middle of them. Sometimes point the dog directly at the articles, other times face away or at an angle to them. A good exercise is to stand in the centre of a circle of cloths, and keep send the dog from different directions. The cloth will remain in the same place each time, but it will be difficult at first, for the dog to know exactly were the correct cloth is, he will get used to working around the circle until he finds it. The dog can become very clever and work this out after a while, so don't repeat it to much and it will be a useful training exercise.

If the dog shows any apprehension or confusion, take him back a few stages, to the start if necessary.

Don't be afraid of repeating the early stages at any time, you are not going backwards but you *are* helping the dog to understand and be confident.

Using scent boards means that you can introduce formality without the dog having the opportunity to go wrong.

Step twenty - Once the dog is ultra confident at all of the above try repeating with a cloth which is not so well used. Start at the beginning of stage eighteen and work through again, rub the cloth well making sure that it has plenty of your scent on both sides. Remember although the dog is able to detect small traces of scent, he is used to having lots on his articles, so we must help him by making sure as much as possible is on the new cloth.

Now we are at the stage where the dog is extremely confident and is working various patterns of cloths, bringing out your scent cloth without a problem, you may wish at this stage to prepare for the ring, if so go to section twenty three. If you are not competing or wish to continue whether you are needing decoy training for the ring or not it will not hurt to go on to stage twenty-one.

Introducing Decoy Scents

Step Twenty-one - Now we will go back to two scent boards only to make the first introduction to a decoy scent. This is a strange scent on one of the cloths that we do *not* want the dog to pick up. In actual fact it is even better if you can take a friend for a walk with you to find the boulders that you used in the early stages, and ask her/him to touch the boulder to put on it their scent. Then you repeat the early stages sending the dog in for your cloth. The new scent introduced is best to be someone that the dog knows and is not afraid of. Thus he will acknowledge the scent and be aware of it, but will not have the opportunity to pick it up. Don't be afraid to tell the dog what you want, help him at any stage. Do not allow yourself to fall into the struck dumb stage, if the dog needs help give it.

This is then progressed to your scent boards, normally I keep a few boards that are specifically for decoy scents, and so the other boards are kept fairly neural. This is not imperative, for training as the dog is learning to find your scent only at this stage, but to simulate ring conditions as much as possible, the cloths that are neutral must remain that way, and fresh decoy scents should be used each time where possible. If you do not have someone with you while you are training then a good substitute will be to use an old decoy, but obviously one that neither you or the dog has touched. As the dog becomes more competent, you will need to ask friends and neighbours for their help. You can ask people to decoy cloths and put them in plastic bags for you to use later, but keep them well away from the other boards and cloths. It is important, to avoid mistakes. The decoy should not available to be picked up by the dog, so it must be attached to your decoy board, but remember you must not touch it!

Step Twenty two - Once the dog is working over the decoy board, more neutrals can be introduced. Build up again as in stage nineteen.

Scent Discrimination

Step Twenty three - When the dog is confidently ignoring your friends scents, both male and female, try introducing a stranger's scent, again starting with only one or two neutrals plus your scent and the decoy. The only scent being *available* to pick up is of course the correct one, yours. It is also worth considering the actual odour of the person in comparison to you. For instance are you a non-smoker or smoker, does your decoy wear perfume or work in a fish factory?

Step Twenty four - You will have spent much time and effort training all of the above stages and once they are competently carried out you will introduce the present and finish, starting with very short recalls, from the scent area on lead to show the dog what is wanted. You will however have been training as part of your retrieve training the retrieve and present of various articles including cloth, so this part can be introduced as a finishing exercise when the dog is able to do the rest of the scent exercise and is almost ready for the ring.

Preparing for Test 'C'

If your are a dedicated trainer and get to enough shows it won't be very long before you need to teach test 'C' scent. Many handlers leave this to the dog and only ever go as far as the above even when the dog is competing in test 'C', they leave the exercise to the dog to work out, working on the assumption that they are teaching the dog to match scents. In training the dog is offered a cloth to take scent from which has the handlers own scent on, and then sent out to match it. This system does work, as has been proved by many handlers. Obedience champions have been created using this tecnnique. This is your choice. Following the experiences of many who have used this technique I have found that once the dog becomes very competent, and has reached the stage where he is no longer learning new things, this matching technique becomes a little too hit and miss, and whilst doing your own scent is very confidence building, if the dog is never in a controlled training situation sent for anything but your own scent, he often reaches a stage where he will start to look for this only. You cannot prevent the dog from taking your scent as well as the judge's in the ring, and so the confusion creeps in. We therefore need to teach the dog to discriminate in a more exact manner.

Step twenty five - A good place to start teaching the dog to go for a scent other than yours is to let a knowledgeable obedience friend or relative do the standard scent with your dog. Only do this if your dog is very happy and used to being handled and played with by the other person. Take the exercise to the basic level, i.e. only the right cloth and a couple of immovable neutrals. Most dogs who have been carefully trained in the basics will have no trouble in adjusting to this. If you

Scent Discrimination

are training on your own or don't feel that your dog would take to this then simply ask someone that the dog knows to put their scent on a couple of cloths for you. Handle them carefully so as not to put your own scent on the cloths, and place one out on a board. Place out a couple of neutral boards, and then hold the cloth in front of the dog and encourage him to smell it. He should by now be very happy *'Smelling'* when told.

Way back at step six you will have started to introduce other people's articles so this will not come as a complete new thing, and of course as you progressed to ring work, the cloths were always someone else's property. You don't need to wrap the cloth around the dog's muzzle or pump his stomach as some people tend to do. You have trained your dog in a very natural manner so far, there is no need to change just because you are hitting the big time! When the dog takes his nose away and is happy with the amount of scent that he has taken, send him out and go with him. He may well go straight to the right one, but help him to make sure, by taking out your cloth letting him have another smell if necessary and encouraging him to collect the right one. Use your key words *'Smell'*, *'Find'*, *'Hold'*, *'Come'*, *'Good boy'*, in the relevant order. Encourage and reward with your voice, make sure the dog knows that he is correct. Use the same person's scent until the dog becomes confident.

Step twenty six - Once the dog understands stage twenty four you can go one of two ways; either you introduce another, different friend's scent for the dog, or you use the same scent and introduce a friendly decoy. The training is exactly the same each time you change something. That is: take it from the beginning, help the dog, aim for success.

Step twenty seven - Now the art of discrimination is really starting to show. The dog can now identify an odour that he knows, ignoring a familiar decoy to bring in the correct scent. Then, on another day the scent roles can be reversed and the dog will competently identify the matching cloth in the scent area. When you reach this stage you are really seeing the dog's nose in action. Eventually you could have all the cloths decoyed, plus the right one and the dog will discriminate. Take it slowly, continue to use the boards to avoid error and don't confuse the scents by fouling or cross scenting them. If you make a mistake go back to the early stages of training and carefully work back up to this stage. You must think about what you are doing. The dog's nose is superb and your job is to educate the dog into how you would like him to use it.

Scent Discrimination

Step twenty eight - It is a simple step now to introduce scents that the dog is less familiar with by allowing the dog to meet someone new for a few moments, and then using their scent. Still as a training exercise, just use two or three cloths on boards to start with, using all of your aids where necessary; voice, lead, etc. It is unlikely by this stage that the dog will have any hesitation, but be ready to help, go out with him, allowing him another sniff of your cloth and encouraging the correct behaviour.

The dog is now able to discriminate between scents. Still take time to do basics, search backs, finding your own scent, informally finding things belonging to other people in the field or garden. Always give him the scent from your hand, an article, cloth, or garment belonging to someone else. Do **not** be indoctrinated into formality, enjoy your dog's skill.

Save the finished article with all the cloths available to the dog for the competition ring.

176

Obedience Training and Show Craft

Section	Page

Clubs

Many people reading this book will be members of dog training clubs, many of which are very good and give a high standard of instruction based on behavioural knowledge and up to date methods. Others promote a style of training which leaves handlers who attend week after week tramping around a hall going through the motions of exercises that although they look fairly accurate, would never win any competitions. Then they wonder why, when they get to a show they are not always in the top six. It is easy to fall into this trap. Inside all of us is a little bit of a show off, and most people who reach even beginner competition standard, are at a very advanced level in comparison to the rest of their club members, and may even be invited to demonstrate or to instruct. This type of training, whilst maybe

serving a purpose for pet handlers, does not usually help your competition standard, and certainly does not increase *'the want'*.

I must impress at this point, that I do not want people to read this and hang up their club subscription for good, far from it, we need good clubs and handlers like you to set an example of what can be attained, but unless your dog is already a workaholic then you should give serious thought to what you are doing out on the club floor.   Analyse whether your efforts are doing any good from the point of view of stimulating high interest and the dog's *'want'* to work with you.

Some clubs are very competitive and offer a high standard of professional style tuition. If you are fortunate enough to join a club whose aims are set high then you are very lucky make the most of it. If your club is more akin to the former, then maybe you can work your way around the situation without upsetting some of our most dedicated trainers. If there are enough handlers keen like you. You could consider starting a class within your club purely for competition work, and ask local competitive instructors, ticket or C handlers to guest instruct, it is even worth offering payment or expenses in order to get the right sort of person to help you. Failing that just have a working session helping each other when the pet classes have finished.

Try to avoid the situation where you feel you must break away from your KC registered club because without clubs we have no shows. If clubs loose people like you, then what have new handlers and enthusiast to look to and aim for? New handlers coming into dog training may never hear of competitive obedience without some one like you to show them the way.

If all else fails you can always go along to socialise and make the tea, or join the committee and help to run things. Instructing is another possibility and there are various bodies who hold excellent courses to help you to learn more about teaching people to train their dogs. They also issue certificates at various levels to show your level of achievement in the form of a qualification.

Avoiding Mistakes

Mistakes in the ring mainly occur through nerves, and the fact that the handler does not perform in exactly the same manner as they do in training. When teaching your dog you must be very careful to ensure that your voice, your body posture, your deportment and your attitude are the same as they will be in the ring. This means careful choice and use of voice and commands/signals. It means learning to remain up right as much as possible when teaching the dog, obviously sometimes you have to be down at dog level to start with, but you should progressively straighten, and aim at the end of the teaching session to be in a good natural upright position to mirror your posture in the ring. The dog cannot be expected to think that their handler waving his body all over the place in training means the same as their handler who stands rigid in the ring. Many handlers make the mistake of not teaching the dog that the exercises are linked one after another when performed in the ring, some may have made the start of an exercise in training different to the start in the ring. This occurs particularly in exercises like sendaway where the handler never goes through the rigmarole of preparing for the start of the exercise as he will be directed by the steward in the ring. On the other hand, only in the ring will the handler fiddle about with the lead, answer or ask questions, keeping the dog waiting to begin. Only in the ring will the handler send the dog straight to a sendaway following heel work or other such exercise. Working like this is bound to create errors and the dog cannot be blamed for you not preparing him correctly for the ring procedure. *(See Only in the ring!)*

As you will of course realise if you have worked through the various sections of the book, we cannot become regimented and perform the exercises as per ring standard and expect the dog to carry on being accurate and precise. This is where the sections on *Linking* and *Routines* will help you and your dog to get into the right frame of mind, and avoid those ring situations that result in the loss of points.

Mistakes in training often occur because the handler does not fully understand what they are trying to achieve. They may not have thought out the exercise fully, or may have failed to break it down into segments that the dog is capable of comprehending. So obviously a complete understanding of the exercise and your teaching procedure is of paramount importance before you begin to train.

Incorrect *Timing* is also a major stumbling block, developing perfect timing takes time, and patience, you must learn to think like a dog to get it right. *Understanding the dog's mind*, explains how the dog relates to things, once you understand this you can then guide, reward, and control situations at the correct time which transforms dog training from a task to a joy.

Correcting Mistakes

It is very difficult for the dog to understand that after being taught something we then want to change part of it. Typically faults occur on heel work for instance, wide working, wide about turns, inaccurate or inconsistent heel position, of course there are many more. Simply correcting the faults when they occur teaches nothing more than the fact that the dog should continually correct himself. This is no good for the ring. Although it might feel to you as though the dog knows where he should be, a dog that has been trained by correction of faults stands out a mile when you are a judge. The dog will be forever weaving his body around, some will be quite wound up over the fact that they must wiggle about until the handler is pleased. Most will assume, (quite correctly), that this is what they have been taught - to take up one position and then change it to another. Of course we see this as an error, justifying ourselves by saying that he knew he was wrong because he corrected himself! Of course we know that if the dog is not in the correct position at any time during the round then this is a markable offence. The fact that he might have corrected himself is quite irrelevant from a judging point of view. Admittedly there might be less points lost than with the dog who does not get into the correct position at all, but never the less there are too many points lost to win the class in most instances.

So where you have faults look at the problem objectively, teach to make sure that the dog understands every part of every exercise. Try to analyse at what point things start to go wrong and retrain the exercise, giving all the help you can to make sure the dog performs in the way that is correct for the ring. Make sure you think carefully about your training and pay attention not only to the part of the exercise that was at fault, but to the whole thing, most particularly to the segment immediately preceding the fault as this will act as a catalyst to trigger the next move.

Only in the ring - Never in training!

One of the most common pleas for help in the world of obedience training stems from the handler getting exactly what they want from the dog in training, but not in the ring, why?

The problems come in varying degrees. Sometimes the team have a problem with a particular exercise, but more often than not the handlers problems start and refer to everything from the minute that they walk into the ring, or even before that in the warm up session. This is such a common problem that the whole of the next chapter has been dedicated to it!

When one or two specific things go wrong on a regular basis.

Years ago a friend confided in me that she felt that if only she could get the superb sendaway in the ring that she was getting in training, she could have easily won the championship class, having come out of the ring twice on the trot, with the points lost on sendaway being the difference between winning and not even featuring in the line up. A most infuriating case of the *'If Onlys'*.

Obviously her training technique was good because the dog was super confident in training, and even when the dog was trained in new surroundings, and in a situation that looked, for all intents and purposes, like a ring. she never failed to do a perfect exercise. Obviously the dog was not understanding something when it came into the show ring, so something was different between the training sessions and the real McCoy!

The handler, although she had achieved this very high standard of obedience was convinced that her dog was being naughty. Of course if you read the section on *understanding the dog* you will know that the dog does not possess the ability to decide to be naughty or vindictive, and certainly is not able to single out one particular thing to keep on getting wrong to prove a point to this human on the other end of the lead. Actions and thoughts like these are human vices and we should honour our four footed friend with more respect.

So, having convinced the handler of the dog's integrity, we set about the task of finding out what the difference was that was confusing the dog. I watched them perform in the ring and then watched them in a training session, and indeed the dog performed as predicted. Then we talked through a typical training session when the handler was away from a show. Obviously the rules were being followed and her training was very thorough. When it came to sendaway she said that they realised the dog should not see them setting up the sendaway markers every time, so they were set up at the beginning of most sessions, even before the dogs were out of the car. The handler trained with a friend of a similar level. They regularly stewarded each other to make sure that they were used to turning, stopping etc. when told, and also they were able to train against this to make sure that the dogs did **not** learn to work to the ring stewards commands. They obviously were

182

tackling things very seriously. On sendaway the handlers said that they called out the steward's commands for each other, and throughout the session, took it in turns so that the dogs didn't get bored. I asked the handler to talk me through her sendaway procedure, not just from the set up but what were you doing before that. It transpired that the handlers were putting the dogs in the car having a coffee and a rest before going onto sendaway, scent and stays. This had become their natural breaking point, So the dog had learned that the sendaway came after she had enjoyed a snooze in the car and that it was never linked to other exercises.

Although we know that the dog does not think backwards and forwards, we also know that the dog's reactions are triggered by each other. In order to perform in a very specific way such as we need in the ring he needs to learn how to sequence and link in the way that we need it. Once the handler learned how to teach the dog to link exercises together in training, she then went out the following week and won the ticket. All her other training had obviously been very sound and it was just a simple chink in the armour that had prevented success previously. It is hard to believe that such a tiny error can cost so much, but once you understand the dog's mind it will all become so very clear to you.

When everything goes wrong!

What do you do when just everything goes wrong in the ring? The dog is totally switched off, and even though he goes through the motions of doing some of the exercises he is no where near as good as he can be in training.

Most handlers will have been told that it is themselves that are at fault. But what use is that for an answer? It just makes you feel totally inadequate, you feel like giving up. What you must do is look at yourself carefully, and try to examine what it is that is different about you and the way that you handle the dog. This might not just be one thing, there may be several answers to the puzzle. At the extreme, handlers have a fit of nerves or fear of being shown up and give all the wrong signals to the dog. So then we have to look at ways of controlling the handler before we can move on to examining the ways in which the dog might perceive the actual situation. Firstly be aware that a judge, in most cases, is just another dog handler taking a day off from competing and doing their bit for the show society.

Every judge is a different person and of course they will all react to their day of judgement in differing ways, but on the whole they are 'human', and most will be able to recall being in a similar position to you. So go in and relax! Easier said then done I can hear you say, but think of the pressure on the other end of the scale when top handlers go into the ring with an audience of people. Some of the audience wanting and expecting them to do well, and some of their fellow

Correcting Mistakes

competitors hoping that they don't! (Are people really like that? Surely not!). So clearly everyone has a certain amount of pressure, it is learning to deal with it that is the important thing. Many handlers find relaxation techniques and yoga very useful and others have turned to herbal remedies to help. Turn to *'Keeping Your Cool'* for more help with this. Then you must make sure that all of the exercises taught to the dog are progressed to the point that will make sense to the dog in the ring. You must make sure that your voice sounds the same, your posture is correct and your footwork is accurate. Many handlers will teach excellent static exercises to the dog and then never combine those with the footwork and correct signals in the ring, and so the dog cannot understand what the handler wants. As you know from personal experience anything that is too complicated for you to understand easily soon becomes boring or is dismissed as beyond you, unless the goal is extremely rewarding. Even then the goal sometimes seems so inaccessible that after a few enthusiastic attempts your tendency, as an intelligent human, is to switch off, or change to something that you can do successfully. So who can blame the dog? He is trying to understand a different species from himself, a foreign language, a different culture, a different life style, a different recreation, and someone keeps moving the goal posts!

To make sure that you are getting it right for your dog read the sections on *understanding, linking, routines, timing,* and make sure that you are following all of the *technique* procedures accurately. Create ring like situations not just for the dog but for you, get a friend to steward you from scratch, event to the point of asking what ring number you have and the name and breed of your dog, 'are you ready', adding anything that a steward might say. That little bit of preparation will make both you and the dog more accustomed to the ring situation, and more relaxed when you enter the ropes.

Only In The Ring!

Many handlers suffer from the *'Only in the ring'* syndrome. This tends to mean that the dog is fine in training but when he gets within the ropes he is a different dog. Mostly the answer lies within the handler. They tend to be, to all intents and purposes, a different person when faced with the stress of the competition. Many handlers get within the ring ropes and race around like a bat out of hell, or try so hard to be controlled that their pace is unnaturally slow or stilted. Not keeping calm, not handling as you have trained, even something simple like not smiling as you normally do in training will throw some dogs. Many handlers are not sufficiently rehearsed in ring technique, and so the dog is unaware of what is going on around him. Handlers will find it difficult to keep the dog, (and themselves) in the right mode when they are not used to being kept waiting by stewards. The concentration level necessary to keep the dog on the boil, must be well schooled and the handler must, as part of the training procedure, teach the dog to switch on and off when and as required.

All of the above are a very necessary part of ring craft. You need help from like minded people to condition yourself into the procedures. It is simple to learn to turn when you are ready, not so simple to turn as told under pressure. You need someone to talk to you at the beginning of an exercise, just as a steward would. Set up role play exercises, pretending that you are at a show. This is beneficial for both you and the dog.

Linking is very important. It is all very well to train each test thoroughly, but the dog and you must learn to go from one exercise to another smoothly with out breaks, and without having to get a toy out in-between. This is covered in the linking section. If you don't learn how to link the dog will not necessarily understand what you are doing next, and even if he manages to get on the right wave length he may have a stilted start.

Spooks

Sometimes things have happened that are beyond your control. The dog may spook at certain instances, objects, or particular types of people in the ring. Maybe a judge inadvertently frightened your dog. Noisy wet weather outfits are one of the main culprits for this. To work on building your dog's confidence you need to use a counter conditioning technique, with distraction training. Find a situation that the dog is ultra confident in and introduce gently and from a distance the object or person that the dog is spooked by. Use your special toy or an especially tasty titbit to teach the dog to play or accept being with the problem, and then gradually bring the problem nearer to the dog. This type of teaching is covered in more depth in my first book *'Every body Can TRAIN Their Own Dog'*.

There is no easy answer only patient training to teach a good association with good occurrences. Try to get the dog in the right frame of mind before he becomes frightened. Avoid the fear being brought on by surprise by choosing your situations in which to train. Fear is far more difficult to deal with for you the handler if you had not anticipated the fear response in your dog. Anticipating a problem means that you can start to steer the dog away, even before the fear has had time to get a hold.

Keeping Your Cool

How easy to say, and how hard for some to do. It is probably equally difficult to keep calm if your are doing a run off for first place in your first beginners, as it is to run off for first place at Crufts. Keeping your composure is so important, because if this goes so does your deportment, your footwork, and your rhythm. Your voice turns to a squeak, and even your body gives off a different odour.

Preparation is the best tool

Before the show you should have got yourself into the habit of turning on a steward's commands. Even if this has to be a tape recording, it is better than not practising at all. You should make sure that you have covered in training all the exercises needed for the test, and all the various pointers covered in linking so that the dog does not get confused when you go from one exercise to the next. Make sure that you have good deportment and that your feet automatically go in a set pattern when you hear the turns called. The more you have practised the less of this you have to concentrate on in the ring, and so it will be more easy to keep calm.

Before entering the ring make sure that you know exactly what you will be wanted to do. By this I don't mean memorise the round, but you should be aware what direction you will be starting in. You should know if there are any specific twists or turns that you should be aware of, or is there an unexpected halt somewhere. In the higher classes what pace will be first, where the first position comes, where the dog is meant to be landing in the sendaway, where the correct scent cloth will be. You should accustom yourself to the steward's voice, and keep an eye on the ring running order so that you are not called from the furthest corner of the show ground because you are last to work your dog.

Before it is your turn spend some time getting yourself and the dog in the correct frame of mind for working, by going through some training routines.

Don't be tempted to go through finished exercises, save the master piece for the unveiling in the ring. Olympic sprinters don't keep testing the finished article, they prepare and train!

Think positive and do some breathing exercises to calm your nervous system down before you start. Keep taking deep breaths as you go in to the ring, and concentrate on your dog and what is being said. Block out everything else, and pretend that you are training with a friend, force yourself to be as normal as possible. If you feel that you prefer to work without a crowd, keep your eye on the ring and when the judge looks as if he is not busy, go over and ask if he would like you to work, even if it is not your turn.

Don't try to hard, some handlers get so strung up in the fact that they have not got that illusive win that they wanted, at the end of the day there is always another dog show, you chose the sport as your hobby, relax and enjoy it.

Show Etiquette

The judge, steward and show officials have given up their day to help you to enjoy yours. They do it for various reasons. Some feel that as competitors they are giving something back when they for go a day's competing to judge or help out. Some want to remain involved in the sport, in-between dogs, or after retiring from competition, and most I hope, do it because they enjoy it.

It is enjoyable to see lots of different dogs performing a test that you as a judge have set. It is a great learning ground, you can certainly see where a lot of handlers make mistakes. You observe the silly mistakes that handlers make that can waste the whole round, sometimes what they do is not related to the dog at all. At one show when I was judging, two handlers in my ring threw things out of their pockets whilst working, presumably because they had become loose or irritating, unfortunately and by coincidence both handlers had thrown the articles to one side of the sendaway box. Guess where their dogs went on the sendaway exercise!

In entering under a judge, or finding yourself in their class when you get to the show, you have agreed to accept their decision, (providing it is within the rules set down by the Kennel Club). It pays in life to be pleasant, smile and the world smiles with you as the old saying goes. Your judge is human too. Even if you find the judges decision hard to take, so long as the rules are followed he is entitled to his opinion, so you might as well grin and bear it. You can always avoid entering under the judge again. If you are really sore send a polite note to the show secretary after the show. If he is a bad judge over all, show societies will learn not to invite them again when people continually ask not to go into their class.

If you feel that the judge has acted outside of the KC rules, then ask for a quiet word with him at the end of your round or when he has a minuet. Give him chance to explain, you may have misunderstood. If you are still not happy then the next step is to have a word with the chief steward, he may be able to help you to iron out any problems, but don't expect him to side with you if yours is a border line case, he will almost always give the judge the final decision. In all situations it pays to keep your cool and be sure of your facts. Always carry a copy of the KC rules so that you can check your facts before you open your mouth and look a fool, refer directly to the rules that you feel are not being adhered to. In extreme cases of misconduct you can make an official complaint to the Kennel Club, and the procedure for doing this can be found in the KC Year Book, available from the Kennel Club.

Going into the ring

When it is approaching the time for your turn, wait near the ring entrance. Make sure the score steward knows in plenty of time, that you are available and waiting. Sometimes handlers will try to, jump the queue by asking the table score steward if they may work. If you see a lot of people around, you may need to point out to the score steward that your number is next on the scoreboard. Sometimes the judge overrules the running order. Usually this happens because he has been kept waiting earlier, or because of bad weather etc., if this is the case you may have to have your name added to the list with the score steward. Be patient. If you feel that your running order is going to clash with your stay exercise or with your running order in another ring, have a word with the judge or score steward. Stays will take priority, and a running order in the first ten, or in championship class will take precedence, after that, but the judge must be informed and the score board marked with your reasons for not attending on time to be on the safe side.

When eventually you are invited into the ring, smile and say hello. Be attentive to anything that the judge or steward have to say. Try as hard as you can to follow the instructions immediately they are given and be as helpful as you can. Politely ask any questions if you are not clear on some point and thank the judge/steward for their help. At the end of the round, thank the judge for the nice round, and the steward for his assistance. If your dog has not faired so well or you have had to help him, thank both the judge and steward for their time.

Make sure that you are at the stay ring *at least* five minutes before the set time. Most stay stewards will want to position you and take your ring number so that they can be ready to start the test on time. It is in your own interests to be there in plenty of time, because then the dog has time to acclimatise to the situation, and with a bit of luck you can chose a good spot, although at some shows you will be told where to stand and this may be in numerical or running order. Be aware that the rules on extra commands and signals apply equally in the stay exercises, and even in the lower classes you will lose your points if you talk to your dog.

At the end of the day check the scoreboard and raise any queries first with the score steward, and then if necessary with the judge. In the lower classes you are almost always told how many points you lost and on what. In the higher classes this is not the case, so it is worth looking at the judge's score sheet if this is made available to you, and checking the master score sheet to make sure that they tally. Even judges make addition mistakes, take it from one who has made a few!

If you do not wish to complete the scent or stay exercises you shouid inform the score steward and ask them to mark the scoreboard accordingly. There is

Show Etiquette

nothing so infuriating for a judge than to have to wait around at the end of the day for someone who has gone home.

Always check the score board at the end of the day, you may have done better than you thought. Every judge will mark faults a little differently. Some will mark every little thing whilst others will mark only major faults. Under some judges for instance the loss of seven points will mean you may as well go home. Under other more critical judges you may end up winning. Judges will be anxious to make sure that anyone in the top six or so receives their prize, make sure that you are there, or that the score steward knows where you are if it is possible that you might be included.

Etiquette at the show is all about following the rules being polite and treating others as you would expect them to treat you, basic life etiquette really. Remember most people go to a show for a day out away from their usual lifestyle, for only a very small minority will it ever be anything more. Most are in the sport for recreation, whatever **your** dreams, intentions or ambitions, try to avoid spoiling some one's day!

Diversification

Mixing the disciplines

Many handlers seem to have a fear of mixing the types of training with the same dog. Particular common phobias are those of mixing conformation showing with competitive obedience for fear that the dog will want to keep sitting in the show ring, and working trials and obedience for fear that the dog will not be able to cope with scent discrimination in obedience, as well as the area search in working trials. There are many handlers over the years who have proved that with careful and well thought out training procedures the dog should not become confused. British handlers seem to be the most fearful with only a comparative handful of handlers currently mixing their sports, and even fewer who have taken their animals to championship or top level in more than one field. There are probably two main reasons for this, one the fear of confusion, but even more the fact that competition is so fierce that all of the handler's energy, money and available time are put into their favoured sport.

Abroad there is more emphasis on promoting the handler's breed as a good 'all rounder', so it more common to see many breeds of dog enjoying all disciplines.

In Britain some breeds are encouraged and this is particularly common in the rarer working type breeds which are imported and then bred in this country.

Within your chosen sport

By the fact that you are reading this book I would naturally assume that one of your main interests is competitive obedience either solely or with other sports. If you are a 'single tracker' and obedience is your only goal do not be afraid to introduce your dog to different things by way of a little light relief. In the section on circuit training I have explained how I use jumps and obstacles to keep things novel and interesting. If you become too single tracked the more laid back dog can become bored and the very wound up dog can become even more so because of the predictability of life. Taking retrieve as an example, the Leonberger for instance, unless you are a very inventive trainer may well reach the stage where he looks at you as if to say 'If you wanted it why did you throw it away?' The Collie on the other hand becomes so hyped up wanting to get on to the chasing part, that

Diversification

he finds it hard to control himself whilst the article is thrown. I am not trying to suggest that by introducing a jump or a tracking session that you will solve your retrieve problems, far from it! But if you refrain from becoming too intense on specific issues, training will become more natural and more of a pleasure for both sides of the team. Even if all you have time for is to teach a few tricks in the home, you will find that the lighter side of training has a good effect on the rest.

Diversification is particularly useful for dogs who have been taught all of the obedience exercises, handlers will find that the minute that they stop teaching new things, the dog starts to become very clever at racing ahead in the things that he knows, this is especially true of the very keen type dogs. If you *never* stop teaching then it keeps you both on your toes, and neither dog or handler becomes blasé.

Obviously time will have a bearing on how much you can dabble in, or even take seriously, the various sports and disciplines, but if you can, make the time to add spice to your dog's life. Understanding how to teach your dog other things will also help you to understand more about dogs. Choose an exercise that your dog may have a natural aptitude for, or that you find interesting, and have a go!

Willow's dad 'Carting', with owner Fred Inwood

Conclusion

Competitive obedience for most people is a hobby. For a few it is a way of earning a little extra, and a minority of people are fortunate in that they have managed to turn their pastime into a business and are able to make their living from the sport or its ancillary branches. Which ever section we fit into, we should all remember that the dog is with us because we so desire, he has no say in the matter, and does not have the choice to walk away.

The dog may not always perform in the way that we might like, but at the end of the day we are the teachers, he is but the pupil, trying to make sense of a foreign world.

Planning for the future will make your training easy, aim high but keep your daily targets low. Don't achieve accuracy at the cost of enthusiasm, you will need both to win tomorrow.

Training is about preparing yourself and your dog, about understanding your pupil's needs and abilities, about enjoyment, and about building up a life long partnership a bond of trust.

Winning is a great feeling, but we must also feel good about ourselves and about the way we achieved that success.

Happy Dogs - Happy Winners
Control the games, have fun with your dog and when it all goes wrong just laugh and try again!

Another day another dog show!

Winning and loosing - at the end of the day the trophies and rosettes take second place to the partner ship. Pat Leverick and her rescue dog Ross of Collali

193

Useful Information

Up-to-date copies of the **Obedience Competition Rules** are available from :
The Kennel Club, 1 Clarges St, Piccadilly. London, W1Y 8AB. Tel 071 493 6651.

Britain's number one magazine solely on Competitive Obedience, Obedience Competitor Magazine, covers obedience shows, show calendar, adverts, reports and events. It is on sale at some Obedience shows and also available by subscription from:
Obedience Competitor Magazine, Long Meadows, Mooredges, Thorne. Doncaster. S. Yorks. DN8 5RY. Tel 0405 740529 Fax 0405 740529.

Angela White holds regular training courses, days, camps, lectures, talks, workshops and individual tuition. She is also available for any of the above at your own club, venue or function world-wide. Contact Michael White on Tel 0405 812144. Fax or write to Angela White PR, c/o the Obedience Competitor Magazine office.

Personally signed copies of Angela White's first book **'Everybody Can TRAIN Their Own Dog'** are available from Obedience Competitor Magazine, at shows or by mail order.

More copies of this book together with Angela White's Troubleshooting booklets, Obedience Record Books, Judges Lists etc. available from Rainbow Publications, Long Meadows, Mooredges. Thorne. Doncaster DN8 5RY.
Tel 0405 812144   Fax 0405 740529

Club and Trade enquires welcome.

More useful information continued over...................

194

Useful Information.......................

Common Obedience Abbreviations

HW - Heel work
DC - Distance Control
HF - Heel Free (off lead)
WAT - Wide about turn
WRT - Wide right turn
POS - Loss of heel position
ASSD - Positions in heelwork
OCP - Off centre Present
ARO - After a run off
WPU - Wide pick up
BEG - Beginner
HS - Head or Hand signal
VCP - Very crooked Present
Surge - Surge out of position
1L - Presenting to one leg
PU - Pick up
Sc - Scent
Drop - Drop of article or cloth
OB CH - Obedience Champion
WS - Working Sheepdog
SS - Shetland Sheepdog
GR - Golden Retriever
BS - Belgian Shepherd

RET - Retrieve
TT - Temperament test
REC - Recall
WF - Wide finish
WLT - Wide left turn
DR - Drift from heel pos
DC - Distance Control
CP - Crooked Present
RW - Ring work
CS - Crooked Sit
POT - Potential
BS - Body signal
LO - Laying on
SS - Slow Sit
Hang - loss of position
Pres - Present
OOS - Out of sight
S - Slow
C - Clear (nothing lost)
GSD - German Shepherd
Aus - Australian Shepherd
Leo - Leonberger
Heinz 57 - Mongrel

SA - Sendaway
HOL - Heel on lead
L - Lagging
WT- Wide turn
W - Wide
POS - Position
ANT - Anticipation
HES - Hesitation
RO - Run off
NOV - Novice
F - Full Marks
XC Extra command
CR - Crabbing
DS - Double sit
Dev - Deviation
Fin - Finish
M - Mouthing
Erat - Erratic
BC - Border Collie
Lab - Labrador
X B - Crossbreed
Terv- Tevereun

Contents

Contents Continued.......

Contents Continued........